# Sorry Not Sorry

# Sorry
# Not Sorry

# ALYSSA
# MILANO

**DUTTON**

**DUTTON**

An imprint of Penguin Random House LLC
penguinrandomhouse.com

LIBRARY OF CONGRESS CATALOGING-IN-PUBLICATION DATA
has been applied for.

ISBN 9780593183298 (hardcover)
ISBN 9780593183311 (ebook)

Printed in the United States of America
1st Printing

BOOK DESIGN BY KATY RIEGEL

*To my David.*

*I'll be your mirror.*

# Contents

# CONTENTS

# Sorry Not Sorry

# Introduction

I started writing this book at the end of 2019. It was going to be nearly an activism memoir, reflections on the passions of my life and the progress I want to be a part of going forward. Just as I made the first keystrokes, a new virus emerged on the other side of the world. Within days, a few news reports trickled in, but it was easy to ignore. The Iowa Caucus and the New Hampshire primary were weeks away. Many candidates had dropped out by that point, and once again my party was fighting a fierce battle over who would square off against Donald Trump, who looked poised for reelection despite his looming impeachment.

And then, in the blink of an eye, the pandemic hit.

Before we really knew what it was, I had it. I spent much of the late winter sure I was going to die, struggling to breathe.

Over the year, my hair began to fall out, I was always exhausted, and I experienced a persistent brain fog. I was terrified that I would give it to my parents, my husband, my kids—and that if I didn't, some careless jerk who didn't take it seriously would. Before long, I forgot what it was like not to be afraid. The security and safety we felt as Americans, that *I* felt, was shattered.

And through that experience, the shared nightmare we all lived or died through, I wrote. It changed what I planned, and how could it not? This book became a snapshot of a year in the life of an activist as everything we knew about the political world and the physical world seemed to devolve around us. An unleashed and unconstrained Donald Trump whipped up a frenzy of hatred and stupidity the likes of which we hadn't seen in this country since the Salem witch trials, all while the novel coronavirus killed hundreds, then thousands, then hundreds of thousands of us. It changed how I see the world and changed how we all live in it.

So this snapshot that you're holding is reflective of the world as it existed when I wrote. Some situations will have resolved by the time you read it—at least I hope they will. Others will spring up in their place. As I write this introduction, Donald Trump is out of office after inspiring an insurrection that got him impeached. Again. We're about to cross five hundred thousand COVID-19 deaths. I worry so much that as you're reading this, it will be a million. Or that one of the variants that are just now emerging will overwhelm the ability of the vaccine rollout that Trump never planned and never executed. But behind that worry is hope. For the first time in years, I have real hope. I believe in the competence of the Biden/Harris administration, and in these early days that faith is already being borne out. I hope that 2021 starts to look materially different from 2020. I hope you're reading this in a world where you're planning a big family Thanksgiving, or out in a restaurant surrounded by people and breathing safely.

But if you're not, I'll be wherever you are, standing beside you. We'll get through what comes together.

*—AJM, January 26, 2021*

# On Being
# Unapologetically Fucked Up

Back in February of 2019, a group of white Catholic school boys attended a march in Washington, DC, celebrating efforts to take abortion rights away from women. While there, red MAGA hats nestled smugly over their heads, they had an encounter with Nathan Phillips, a Native American man who had been participating in an Indigenous Peoples March. While the events that led to this confrontation are in some dispute, the images and recordings of part of it are shocking. As Phillips approached the crowd of boys while chanting and beating a traditional drum, some of the boys, laughing, appeared to mock Phillips with chants and tomahawk chops. One student named Nicholas Sandmann, wearing a MAGA hat and standing just a foot away, locked eyes with Phillips for several minutes while holding a derisive and smug grin, and though he made none of the racist gestures of the boys with him, many people interpreted his actions as part of the broader racist behavior. There are two sides to every story, but only one side is right in this one—and it isn't the boys'.

I wrote an op-ed about it for *The Wrap*, called "Red Hats Are the New White Hoods—Let's Take a Stand." To say the article pissed off a few people would be the understatement of the century. A whole lot of fragile white men lost their collective shit. Several of the students filed lawsuits over reporting on this incident. Sandmann sued six media outlets and threatened numerous lawsuits, including against me personally even though everything I said was clearly visible to anyone who saw the video. I don't know what his motivations were with Phillips, but the chanting and gesturing fools this boy came with made their motivations quite well-known by virtue of that red hat, a symbol of American racism, sexism, bigotry, hate, and oppression since 2015.

What follows are not opinions; they are facts. In the 1920s, Fred Trump was arrested at a Klan rally. Contemporaneous reporting from multiple sources makes it easy to deduce that Fred Trump was one of the Klan members and not a bystander: seven people were arrested; Fred Trump was arrested; all seven people arrested were described by the police as "berobed." Those dots are not hard to connect. Fred and his son Donald were sued over racial discrimination under the Fair Housing Act in the 1970s. Fred was so racist Woody Guthrie even wrote a song about "old man Trump" and his "color line." Donald himself took out a full-page ads in four New York City newspapers calling for the death penalty for the Central Park Five—unjustly accused teenagers who were later proven to be completely innocent. As a candidate and as a president, he's said racist things, promoted and enacted racist policies, stoked racial hatred, employed confirmed white nationalist Stephen Miller, called on the white nationalist Proud Boys to "stand back and stand by," and attacked the Black Lives Matter movement and its members. Donald Trump is a racist. It's part of his brand. In my view, it's not disputable.

That is fucked up.

This incident, with these white, entitled children demonstrating all of the isms at once, one of whom leveraged his many privileges into victimhood, demonstrates so clearly what is fucked up in so many aspects of society. Sandmann and his family claim that it was a chaotic situation, but their actions were still unapologetically fucked up. Despite all of the privileges they, and especially their son, enjoyed—race, gender, sufficient wealth to afford private school, education, social status, religion—they somehow made themselves the victims, to the tune of at least two legal settlements. It viscerally turns my stomach. Instead of taking this opportunity to teach their son to be a better man, to be open and expansive and evolved, they doubled down on their entitlement *and got paid for it.*

Fuck.

In 2013 the Supreme Court threw out key provisions of the Voting Rights Act. John Roberts, a year after Trayvon Martin was murdered and a year before Michael Brown was killed, said "our country has changed." In the years that followed, leading into the 2018 midterm elections, Southern states—those that had been previously regulated by the Voting Rights Act—closed more than twelve hundred polling places, mostly affecting the poor and voters of color. By early 2019, seven counties in Republican-led Georgia had only *one* polling place. Voters had to wait hours in line, and some were forced to cast provisional ballots even though they had been in line long before the polls closed. In 2020 the Republican governor of Texas limited drop boxes to one per county. Texas has counties that are bigger than entire states. The Republicans weren't even trying to hide their racism and voter suppression anymore.

*That* is fucked up. And they sure aren't apologizing for it. In fact, they keep trying to make it worse.

Twenty twenty brought a global pandemic to America. The science evolved, but it was clear from the outset: Do certain things like wear masks and keep a few feet away from each other, and the virus was less likely to kill you. And somehow, that became political—okay, not "somehow," it was because an idiot in the White House decided he'd make "live free or die" a literal statement and stupidly equated not wearing a mask with freedom. But as the caskets piled up and virtual funerals became a thing sweeping the nation, instead of saying, "Oh shit, I really blew this and we need to do better to save lives," people decided to double and triple down on their idiocy. Hundreds of thousands of people are dead as of this writing, and most of them didn't need to die. *That* is fucked up.

We had a sexual superpredator in chief appoint three Supreme Court justices. That's fucked up. One of those justices has a credible accusation of sexual assault himself. That is fucked up. There are women who defend both of them. *That* is fucked up. And there are men who want to be like both of them. That is even more fucked up. I'd like an apology for all of it, but it's not forthcoming.

In the last few years, we've seen ICE and CBP agents stop an ambulance that was driving an immigrant child to the hospital for emergency surgery and detain her. We've separated thousands of kids from their parents and locked them in for-profit prisons—run by companies that gave hundreds of thousands of dollars to a presidential inauguration committee. Companies that pay for play in the criminal justice system, profiting off of keeping Black and brown people behind bars. And instead of apologizing for the shittiness of everything that they are, they put out annual reports touting their profiteering on human misery. So fucked up.

Trayvon Martin. Tamir Rice. Michael Brown. Akai Gurley. Breonna Taylor. John Crawford. Rayshard Brooks. Daniel Prude. Atatiana Jefferson. Aura Rosser. Stephon Clark. Philando Castile. Alton Sterling. Freddie Gray. Sandra Bland. Eric Garner. Tanisha Anderson. George Floyd. And on and on and on. That's fucked up.

The fact that some years there are as many mass shootings as days is fucked up. That forty thousand people every year die in America from guns is fucked up. The reality that the gun industry has so badly manipulated the political system and convinced politicians that these deaths are the cost of their blood money is especially fucked up, and not one of those assholes is apologetic. They have no shame.

Beyond the political, though, there is so much more. There's life. There's me.

I deal with generalized anxiety disorder. There are times when I can't function, when my insides turn to churning water and my breath comes in tight, jagged heaves. When my ability to function, to do any of my jobs, is ripped away by the stunning pressure of its sudden onslaughts. When the societal expectation is to function anyway, when I am less likely to be believed about my suffering because I am a woman, and when the bias against this medical condition is persistent throughout the United States. I have to take pills every day, and probably will for the rest of my life, and this medical condition makes me a target for bullies, trolls, and weak men. Yet even when I feel like I can't, I do my very best to work through it, and I will never apologize for my condition or my work as an activist.

I grew up very differently from most Americans. From about as young an age as I can remember, I was working. I'm forty-eight years old, and I've had a forty-year career. I almost never went to a normal school—my schools were tutors on sets between takes. I had to learn most of what I know through my own curiosity, my own fuckups, and my own drive to be better. Because the world is strange, I've been a millionaire since I was nineteen, and I know that gives me a skewed perspective on the world. But I also know it doesn't make me any better than any other person. I know that my job pays a fucked-up amount of money, and conversely that teachers and nurses and cashiers get paid a fucked-up amount of money too.

But those experiences also made me much of who I am today. I will always use the platform that luck and skill and work have afforded me. One of my very favorite things to do is to give my microphone over to people who have important and special things to say, and those who are fighting every day to make the world a better and more just and more equal place. Frankly, the fact that these people don't have platforms of their own on the scale that I do is fucked up, and for that I am really sorry. But I won't apologize for sharing mine. Not once. Not ever.

What I know is that fucked up is as fundamental a state of the world as night and day. I know that utopia does not exist, that there is no attainable or universal perfection while we live and breathe. But I know there is better. I know that "less fucked up" is a state we can live in. It's something I can make happen. And it's a thing worth working for, worth fighting for, no matter how loudly and wildly and stupidly the forces of fucked-upness fight back. And so I fight—against injustice, against my own mental illness, against my privilege and that of others, and against the things that are wrong in the world. Because I never want to see a smug grin on the face of my son as his racist friends make asses of themselves behind him. And for that, I will always be unapologetic.

# Believe Women

When I sent my #MeToo tweet in 2017, I did it from a place of support and love and anger. As he was for so many women who are the victims of sexual assault, Harvey Weinstein was the last straw. Learning these things about this garbage human, how he treated women I knew and loved, filled me with both bone-crushing sadness and soul-burning fury. And so I spoke out in support of Rose McGowan, but also in support of myself and of my daughter, and of the millions upon millions of women around the world who have been or who will be victims of sexual violence. For too long, nobody listened to us. And when they did, they usually didn't believe us.

Nowhere was this more evident than in the amazing work of Tarana Burke, who, unbeknownst to me at the time, had started the #MeToo movement years earlier. She's been in the trenches fighting this fight for years, and one of the greatest gifts of my life has been the opportunity to help lift up the work she's done fighting for women who have been harassed and assaulted by men, and were rarely believed when they told their stories.

In those first days and months after that tweet, it was an avalanche. In every industry, in every country of the world, men who had for so long taken advantage of their societal power for sexual gratification were outed and fell. Some were men I had previously respected and supported. This is not, and has never been, a partisan political movement for me. Nope, not for a minute. And it never will be. This has been about shifting the culture away from *not* believing women who tell their stories into a place where we listen and evaluate and act based on the evidence.

Maybe I haven't done the best job in explaining this distinction—that believing women doesn't mean we believe every word every woman says just because she is a woman. I mean, I sure as hell don't believe everything Kellyanne Conway says, and I shouldn't. When the available evidence contradicts what women say—whether it's about sexual assault or whether it's about kids in cages—of course we don't believe them. Women aren't immune to lying, and nobody ever meant that we should believe women blindly.

What I do mean, and what is really, really important for us

to say, to share, to tell all of the people in our lives, is that we can no longer start with the idea that women are lying. The way women have been treated around sexual assault? It is fucked up. We know that women are routinely gaslit by their abusers. I know so many women, people I love, who were physically, sexually, and emotionally abused by men yet still believe it was their fault. Not because it didn't happen, but because the predators in their lives manipulated, guilted, and abused them into changing their own lived history just to end the cycle of violence. So imagine overcoming that, overcoming the conditioning and the fear and the pain that always, always come with this kind of abuse, reporting it, and getting the *same* treatment from the authorities you talked to.

This next part will be almost as hard for you to read as it is for me to write.

I know of a woman—and I am changing some details here to protect her, but the gist is true—who went to the police after her husband choked their teenage daughter, threw her on the ground, and dumped a bookcase over both of them. He left them bruised and terrified and refused to leave the house. As she and her daughter huddled on the floor of the bedroom, the bookcase pushed up against the door to keep him from getting in, she thought back on so many similar episodes. She thought back on the times he'd raped her, and how his sister had said, "Oh, that's Chad, he didn't mean anything by it," when my friend told her what happened. She remembered the decades of affairs, of being told they were her fault. The financial abuse, the abuse of their children, the constant belittling and hurting and shaming and *breaking* of her center. She saw her daughter crying in her arms, terrified of the man who was her father, and she thought back on the years that perfect girl had been abused. The rage that came from those memories forged a little bit of steel in her shattered core. She vowed to leave and to get help. Eventually they snuck out, and with the support of friends and other people who loved them, she decided to file a report with the police. Do you know what the first question they asked her was?

"What did you do to provoke him? You must have done something."

Can you imagine that? For most of us—although absolutely not all of us—going to the police means safety. It's where we go when a situation gets so dangerous that we know we need protection, and they are our safe haven. Except for women who have been abused physically or sexually, it just too often hasn't been.

She moved back into the house the next day. He is still abusing her. She doesn't see the point in doing anything about it anymore. She wonders what she did to provoke him and cries on the floor of their bathroom when he finally falls asleep.

You know that scene in *A Christmas Story* when Ralphie writes his teacher an essay talking about how he wants a Red Rider BB gun for Christmas? And he's certain that his writing is so clear, so passionate, and so persuasive that she'll have to side with him? Well, instead she writes, "You'll shoot your eye out," on the page. He felt like his mother got to the teacher first, and the two conspired against him. Now imagine that instead of a BB gun, Ralphie wanted to stop being abused, and the teacher acted the same way. That's what the police did to my friend. That's what they do to so many women.

Is there something about a vagina that means women cause trouble? Do men really think that? Because that's how the patriarchy works. They blame us for their own failings. They force us to doubt our own lives, our own history, and our own values. They offer refuge, only to take it away when it is needed most. And as women, we're blamed for seeking that refuge, for rejecting it, and for anything in between. It's a no-win situation, and I'm sick of losing.

I want to talk a little bit about Christine Blasey Ford and Tara Reade. These two women have been shredded by the political machine, their characters, pasts, and motivations held up to scrutiny beyond anything that most of us can comprehend. Their stories, and the situations that created them, put women in an impossible position. We're asked over and over again to absolve perpetrators or potential perpetrators, and to be the arbiters of what's true and what isn't. This is *not our job*. We didn't create the problem, so why are we forced to solve it? These stories came on opposite sides of a political divide, one during a presidential campaign, and that amplified the pressures on women in ways we can't even measure.

We're forced to make pragmatic choices, to accept access to power by working with people who have or may have done terrible things, or to stay on the fringes and retain perfect ideological purity. We're held tight by knots of male creation, and any way we struggle pulls them tighter. Until we break the ropes themselves, it's going to get more and more uncomfortable. In a perfect world, we could have broken those ropes by nominating and electing a woman to replace Donald Trump, the pussy-grabber in chief. But we don't live in a perfect world. The Electoral College tells us that the white men of Pennsylvania and Michigan and a few other places will decide who the president is, and they aren't voting for women. So we're stuck in this trap, pushing like hell to find the way through, not just the way out.

I was on set when I first heard the name Brett Kavanaugh, at least as far as I can remember. It sickened me that Trump got to put another one of his cronies on the Supreme Court, and I soon learned that he was insanely antichoice, he had a history of recommending terrible policy when he served as part of the George W. Bush administration, and he was yet another rich white man who attended private school and was going to be deciding what I could do with my body. I hated it. I vowed to fight against his nomination with everything I had. He was one of the worst possible nominees for the job, and it was time to gear up for war. I'm not hiding that fact at all. Brett Kavanaugh needed to be stopped from joining the court if at all possible.

But never, never in the world would I condone fabricating false accusations against a man for political gain. Not once. If Christine Blasey Ford's story did not have so much corroborating evidence, and so much consistency, I would not have supported bringing her accusations into the Senate hearings until such evidence came forth. But it was there, from the start. She told the same story, consistently, over the years. She told it to a therapist, who had notes verifying it. She told it to her husband. She spoke about the attack to friends over the years. The details remained consistent. She took and passed a polygraph. She did not set out to talk to the press or make her story public—she sent a letter to her senator when she learned this man could end up on the court. And the letter leaked.

Still, under the glare of the lights, her story remained consistent. She talked under oath about her experience. She did not have a political agenda; she had a patriotic agenda. I looked at the totality of the evidence, from the point of view of believing she had a right to be heard and that we had a duty to hear her. This process played out in the very definition of due process: an official hearing. And after listening to what she had to say, I believed her. Unfortunately the Senate did not. I don't know how they didn't. I was in the room when she testified. I heard the ring of truth in her voice. I don't know how anyone who was in that room could not have heard the same thing.

Now, just as I was opposed to Brett Kavanaugh's nomination to the court, I have supported Joe Biden's campaign for the presidency. I've known Joe for quite some time. With me, he has never been anything but warm, kind, friendly, and smart. He comes from a family like mine, where physical affection is the norm, and he's admitted that he may have been too affectionate with women he's encountered. There was no hint of sexual abuse or gratification in the stories of any of the people who have spoken about these kinds of encounters with him, and he's owned up to them. In fact, he's been the example of how a man should handle these things—by listening, promising to keep listening, and changing his behavior to reflect his new understanding. It's exactly what I want from the # MeToo movement. I want men to do better. Joe's doing better. I know him to be a good man. But if I believed he had sexually assaulted a woman, I'd be shouting from the rooftops that he needs to step down.

I have not heard Tara Reade's story in the same light as

Christine Blasey Ford's. As of late 2020, she has not testified under oath. But I believe just as strongly that we have the exact same responsibility to hear, and to honestly vet, her story that we had with Dr. Ford. I know that we need to do this with an open mind and an open heart. We *cannot* start from the position that she is not being truthful, and despite all of what I just said about Joe, I have done my damnedest to make a fair evaluation. In this case, I am really concerned that her story has changed so much. I'm even more concerned that she didn't start telling it as a story of sexual assault until she started loudly supporting his opponent in the primary. I don't like that she claims to have filed a complaint against Biden when she worked for him, but no record of this complaint appears to exist, and I have a hard time with the fact that she's provided a vague enough timeline that Joe can't look at his Senate schedule and have the opportunity to clear his name.

In this case, I've listened and looked at the evidence, and I have a hard time accepting her version of events. But get this: It is a rolling, fluid state. Evidence could come forward that, despite all of these concerns I have, will change my mind. I could learn new information, and new information makes us reevaluate our world, our beliefs, our prejudices. If we are honest with ourselves, if we really, really dig in and look in the mirror, we have to change to match the real world. And if the evidence requires me to do so, I'll change my mind on this. I am always open to the act of believing women. Even women whom I have not believed in the past.

Ultimately, only two people know the truth of what either of these women have to say. Both of them will suffer for telling these stories. And right off the bat, too many people just presumed they were lying. It pisses me off. When we admonish people to believe women, it's that assumption we're trying to erase. Despite what you may think, I did not default to not believing Tara Reade. I didn't default to believing Christine Blasey Ford. I *did* start from a place that allowed for the possibility that each of their stories was true.

Somewhere south of me, across a canyon and a desert, through streets normally packed tight with standstill traffic, my friend is probably hiding somewhere in her house, afraid. So is your friend. Don't you miss her spirit? Don't you remember who she was before she was presumed guilty? Don't you wish we started with the possibility of believing her story?

Maybe we'd still have her.

I believe women.

# The Imperfect Ally

There is an inescapable truth to being an ally: You do not truly understand the experiences of the group you are standing in support of. And you never will. You can't—that's the definition of being an ally: You're outside that group, having different lived experiences, never having to worry about the things the people you are supporting worry about. If you did, you wouldn't be an ally, you'd be living it. And because you can't understand, and you never will understand, you're going to get it wrong sometimes, if not often.

You have to be okay with getting it wrong, hearing that you got it wrong, and committing to doing it better. Being an ally, a true ally, means getting comfortable with being uncomfortable. It means acknowledging your own blind spots, diving into your own failings, and owning every last bit of them. It means feeling the failure, feeling the embarrassment and shame that comes with it—but then turning it into a positive instead of giving up. It's a damned hard thing to do. But it's so important.

In a coming chapter I'll talk about one time I got it wrong, but it certainly wasn't the only time. And I'll probably keep getting things wrong as long as I use my voice. But hopefully in smaller and smaller ways, as I continue to do the work of listening, reflecting, understanding, and acting. And if there's one big lesson I can impart on being an ally, imperfect at it as I am, it's this: Do the work.

Being an ally isn't showing up at a parade with a sign and then going home with a sense of personal accomplishment. Being an ally isn't showing up at a demonstration outside a statehouse, chanting the same chants you chanted at the last demonstration, and then meeting up at a Starbucks after to talk about how you really did some good that day. That's the easy part of being an ally. And if we center ourselves in our reflections, if we focus on the good work we did instead of the hard work we still have to do, we've failed in our jobs.

Let's consider Black Lives Matter for a minute.

First of all, it's a statement. A powerful statement that shouldn't have so much power and meaning behind it. There should, in a perfect world, be nothing political or weighted or controversial about saying "Black lives matter." It's a statement of truth. It's a statement of values. It's a statement that should be universal, not only expressed with our words but manifested in our reality. When we expand on Black Lives Matter by adding "Trans" or "Women's" before "Lives," it should not make it any harder to express support for the movement or the terms that describe it. But so many are unwilling to say it in the first place. And that's where being an ally starts.

I think about Ryan White all the time, and my journey into activism.

In the 1980s, a teenager named Ryan White contracted HIV from a blood transfusion. If you're younger than thirty-five or so, you won't know how terrifying those words were back then. HIV, which people mostly thought of as AIDS, the condition HIV can cause, was a death sentence, and so many Americans didn't understand how it was transmitted. It played into our own fears and hatred, and we behaved as terribly as you'd expect. We took it out on the LGBTQ community, regardless of their HIV status.

It was a scary time to be a teenager, coming of age when sex felt deadly. And if it was frightening for me, it was terrifying for Ryan. It was also lonely and so very sad for him and others who lived with HIV or AIDS. This was the state of the world on the day I received a life-changing phone call. Ryan White wanted me to come on *The Phil Donahue Show*—which was the *Oprah* of its day—and kiss him to prove you can't get AIDS from casual contact.

And I said yes.

Now, I don't want to pretend that saying yes was easy for me. I knew the truth about HIV and AIDS, I understood what the scientists told us about the disease and how it was transmitted, and I understood that kissing Ryan on the cheek was a safe thing to do. But in my guts, in my secret heart, I was *afraid*. I had the prejudices that everyone else had. I had grown up hearing about this disease, how it was somehow immoral, how it was somehow a punishment, and how it was dangerous. Not from my family, but from the world around us. It was the first time I truly had to look deep into myself, see what was causing that fear, recognize my own failings, and work to overcome them.

This was not an easy thing for a teenager—especially a teenager who had been so blessed as me—to do. Teenagers are by nature the stars of their own world. When you're trying to figure out how to be a self-sufficient human in your own right, stepping into the light for someone else is daunting for so many. And it was daunting for me. I wasn't scared—at all—of Ryan or contracting his disease. I was proud to be able to help him. But this was my first step into the world of shining more light on others than on myself, and that was dizzying. I had no idea how much it would come to define my later life, but I did have the sense that it was a precipice and a catalyst for change.

And what became clear in the days and weeks afterward was how freeing it was to let all those fears go. It was freeing to replace that fear with love. It was an emancipation from my own prejudices and an invitation for something that could glow, and grow, and not only make the world better but make me better. I found in that place of transformation and progress and confrontation and discomfort in myself an invitation to a better me. The fear of HIV/AIDS and the social problems it caused were nearly as deadly as the disease itself. But if fear was part of the sickness, love was part of the cure.

And I found that to be equally true for the next thirty years to come.

Part of being a good ally is refusing to react. I'm a baseball fan. More than a fan—baseball is part of the very fabric of who I am. There's nothing like spending three hours on a summer evening listening to the roar of a crowd, the sharp wooden crack of a well-hit ball, and the Dodgers beating anyone who comes to town. One of the things I think sets the pro ballplayer apart from a Little Leaguer is knowing which pitches you shouldn't swing at. Sometimes you have to take a strike to learn who you are as a player. You have to see the pitch coming fast and inside and not charge the mound. Sometimes you realize you're crowding the plate, and sometimes you realize that other people *think* you're crowding the plate—and often those are the same thing. Taking a breath after a close strike, after an inside pitch, and reflecting on what you've learned about the pitcher makes you a better hitter.

Taking a breath when being confronted with a hard truth about yourself will make you a better ally. Not taking a breath leads to "not all men," and "blue lives matter," and all of these other bullshit trends that attempt to usurp the language of causes to bury their purpose. You are going to feel defensive when you are called out. I sure do. It's something that is innate to who we are. When we feel threatened, we react. But the cool thing about being human, the point of being sentient, the thing that separates us from the creatures who hunt at night and live on instinct, is our ability to suppress our base nature, our worst instincts, and act in a way that makes sense in society.

There's a story in the Bible I think of often when I need guidance as an ally. It's the story of Shimei, the son of Gera. Shimei and David were not so sympatico at the beginning: Shimei cursed God and David and generally everything around him. There was division and enmity between the two, but David, as a wise king, let it be. Later, we find Shimei coming to David in full knowledge of his blasphemy and begging forgiveness: "For your servant is conscious of his sin: and so, as you see, I have come today, the first of all the sons of Joseph, for the purpose of meeting my lord the king" (2 Samuel 19).

David's advisers try to have Shimei executed for his sins; David refuses, accepting the reconciliation. Here in this moment of reflection, there can be peace and alignment and friendship between two people divided.

Now, there's another part of Shimei's story that I also reflect on. Shimei made his commitment to David to be a loyal subject and abide by his word. And for twenty years, he appeared to do so, and he and the royals were cool. But then, Solomon, who was the son of David and now king, told Shimei to build a house and stay there. Shimei built the house, but when some of his slaves escaped to a nearby town, he left to reclaim them. Solomon learned of his disobedience, his betrayal of his promise—one of many—and Solomon had him executed.

Shimei said words of commitment, but he did not hold them in his heart. He did not live by the promises he made. And they came back to haunt him.

As allies, we need to keep our promises. They must be durable, and they must be sacrosanct. If we don't hold to them when they are inconvenient, when we think nobody is looking, when they get in the way of our own privilege, then they are meaningless. Worse than meaningless, they undo the goodwill we build together and set ourselves and other allies—not to mention the groups we purported to support—back further than we were when we made the promises. We have to be accountable not only to our partners, but to ourselves. I know I keep coming back to this, but it's so important: We have to be comfortable with being uncomfortable.

I'm not the perfect ally. I'm not trying to lecture you here. I'm just examining the times I got it wrong and trying to prepare you for doing the same. Don't let the discomfort deter you from doing what you know is right. Don't let the criticism you'll receive from your partners deter you—learn from it. Swim in it. Absorb the things that are earned, try to understand the things that are not, and use all of the information you glean to do better. To fail differently. To help.

Because that is what being an ally is about—helping someone else. Helping someone with a lower level of privilege than you achieve an equal level of privilege. It is *never* about you. It is *never* going to be about you. And if you find yourself in the Starbucks after the rally thinking about the good work you did instead of the good work you helped someone else do, you're never going to get better at it. There is honor in helping. There is achievement in standing aside so the sun can shine on the people you've been blocking. There is reconciliation in surrender. And there is a better world on the other side, if we can just get out of our own way.

# David

People often break out the old cliché "Love means never having to say you're sorry." Boy, do I call bullshit on that. Love, in many ways, is a constant state of apology. It means recognizing the things that you fail at, knowing that the person you love sees them too, and trying so hard to be better at them.

But most important, it means being loved in return even with those shortcomings. It means that the apology is usually accepted, and it's usually sincere. Love is not a casual "sorry." Love is making amends. Love is forgiveness. Love is success and failure. Love is perpetual apology.

It's hard building a life with an actor. Very little production actually happens in Los Angeles anymore. If you're cast in a show, you could have to spend months on end in Atlanta or Toronto or Vancouver or just about anywhere *but* Los Angeles. But Hollywood is still the nexus of the entertainment industry, and the work my husband, David Bugliari, does as a talent agent and dealmaker keeps him there. This often means long periods apart for us, and that sucks. We met on the set of a movie I was filming, and by the time we married in 2009, I knew there was nobody else for me. But even then, it was hard for us to navigate a new life together when so much of it was spent apart. I mean, there are benefits to it—there's something to the adage that absence makes the heart grow fonder, and the distance forced us to communicate more and be creative in that communication. Each time one of us leaves, it's almost like dating again, scheduling talks and having long-distance dinner dates. But the added pressures and complications of managing a household on top of managing our relationship while thousands of miles apart is not easy.

But we did it.

Love means you can suggest a national sex strike, and your husband doesn't run away screaming. Let me tell you, if you're ever looking to test your relationship, just suggest women withhold sex until political change is achieved. If you don't see a cartoonish cutout in the front door with a trail of footprints disappearing into the horizon, you've maybe got yourself the real thing.

Love is not a box of chocolates.

By the time you've built a life with someone, you know what you're going to get. There are not a lot of surprises, and when there are, they're usually not great. I know too many people who have lost their relationship to a surprise. A surprise mistress. A surprise debt. A surprise illness. Infatuation loves surprises. Love exists in the absence of them. Love exists in the steady, forward pace of forever. Love overcomes routine, crushes boredom. Love is a conversation over something stupid on TV when you've been together ten years and you're still laughing. The surprise is the love, its endurance, its tenacity. When you think you have nothing left to say and can still have a conversation without wanting to stick your fingers in your ears, that's love.

Love does not need you to be the bread or the knife, the crystal goblet or the wine. Love is bedhead and morning breath—not on the first morning you wake up together, but on the last. Love kisses you anyway. Love might tell you to brush your teeth later but kisses you first. A whole lot of people think love is lingerie. It's not. It's wearing a Chewbacca onesie while you're folding their underwear and knowing they still want you. It's a morning painting alone in the sun while they take the kids skiing. Love is a mermaid snow sculpture built for your kids while you are warm inside.

In relationships, people often describe their partner as

"their rock." I get it. Rocks are solid, steady, grounded, firm in reality. They are something you have to work very hard to break most of the time. They have weight, and they can anchor things to the world. But David is not my rock. He is my magnet.

Like magnets, when partners are misaligned, love can repulse, shoving them away from each other no matter how much they want to be together. But when they are aligned the right way, when you've done the work to get the positive lined up with the negative, they form a bond that is so powerful, so strong, so safe, that almost nothing can pull it apart.

David's and my lives are full of positive. Our lives are full of negative. It would not have taken much, so often and so early on, for those poles to face the wrong way and send us shooting away from each other. But somehow, with work and faith and love and forgiveness and patience, we lined each other up just the right way. We are bound together, a bond that is going to take something stronger and harder than anything we've faced to sever.

Good love, healthy love, electromagnetic love. It apologizes. It binds. It endures and folds and always, always wants to be better. And because of love, it can be.

# The Strange
# World of Campaigns

H unter Thompson wrote *Fear and Loathing on the Campaign Trail '72* beginning in late 1971. In the book, he expounded on his hatred for Richard Nixon while cataloging the self-destruction of the Democratic Party's attempt to oust that terrible president. One of the most bizarre bits of that book—written originally as a series of articles for *Rolling Stone*—is an interview with Richard Nixon in which the two men, mortal enemies, bond over a discussion of football, of all things.

That book has nothing on the real deal.

Back in 2004, when I was still dipping my toe into the world of campaigning, I took a personal, under-the-radar trip to New Hampshire just before the primary. It was cold, but if you've never been in New Hampshire before a primary, it is bursting with energy. Icy air did not deter roving, sign-holding crowds from marching up and down the streets of Manchester. Candidate buses drove slowly down the length of Elm Street— which several people told me that day was the "longest double-ended dead-end street in America"—turned around, and made the drive back the other way. Satellite trucks took up far more than their allotment of parking spaces, and the townies pre-tended to hate it while simultaneously eating it up, usually from the windows of the nearest Dunkin' Donuts. There was a line far out the door of a small diner; every once in a while a candidate would come out, shake every hand down the way, and hop onto one of the passing buses. Everyone shook hands, but most of the time when they left, the people in line would expound on why they would never vote for that bum.

In the afternoon, I went into an event at a downtown Manchester theater, a little bit to get out of the cold and a little bit to see Howard Dean, who was the speaker that day. It was just after his Iowa debacle, where he yelled, "Heee-yaaaaah," to a group of tired and dejected supporters who saw him place third after working hard to place first. What a mon-ster, right? He was getting killed in the media for it, and the "Dean Scream" had the campaign floundering. But he had in-teresting things to say and had so much progressive energy behind his campaign. And it was rare, even for celebrities, to get really up close and personal with a contender for the presidency.

When I got to the door of the theater, a young volunteer asked me my name. Not wanting to lie, but also not wanting to out myself, I told her my name was Jayne. I mean, my middle name is Jayne, and if she heard "Millen" as my last name, well, I guess I just didn't enunciate enough. She added me to a list and handed me a small pack of playing cards adorned with Howard Dean's face—the "Dean Deck," it was called—and I went to take my seat. The hall would have been small for Los Angeles but was, I imagine, large for New Hampshire, and it lent the event a cozy, intimate feel. The plush red seats with hard, slightly curved backs reminded me of the movie theaters of my youth. The room filled quickly, with an excited hubbub echoing, building from the balcony and picked up all the way to the orchestra: Al Franken had walked in and taken a seat not too far away from mine. It was four years before he ran for the Senate, but political buzz was already surrounding him. Not sure if he knew me, I scrunched down into my jacket to preserve my anonymity.

When the lights dimmed, the crowd started chanting: "How-ARD, How-ARD!" A spotlight illuminated the center of the stage, and it was not Howard Dean who first walked out, but the president of the United States—at least, once a week on NBC. Martin Sheen was there to announce Howard, and you would have thought it was the height of Beatlemania from the screaming crowd. I soaked it all in. This was not the kind of environment we got in California, where most people probably never saw a candidate except for on television. The retail politics adage was starting to make sense to me, as the power of talking to voters face-to-face and getting firsthand exposure to issues that actual people were confronting was revealed. Of course, the voters of New Hampshire are not at all like the voters of California or Mississippi, and giving them too much of a say is its own problem, but the connection with *people* was powerful.

When Martin announced Howard Dean, the place again exploded with cheers. Camera flashes, television cameras, press, and supporters all were part of the cacophony. It took Howard a few minutes to get everyone settled down just so that he could work them back up.

It was about twenty minutes into his speech when it happened.

Lyndon LaRouche was a jerk. He was a convicted fraud, was a cult leader, was a disinformation spreader about HIV/AIDS, had contacts with the Klan, and was just a general bad actor. He was also a New Hampshire native and a constant presidential candidate dating back to the seventies. And if La-Rouche was bad, his supporters were even worse. Seriously, take the cultiest Ron Paul supporter you ever met, cut their intellect in half and double their paranoia, and you get a La-Rouchist. You might have seen them in small, self-important, foul-smelling clutches around train stations at rush hour, holding pictures of President Obama and others with Hitler mustaches. Yeah, those idiots. Well, unbeknownst to everyone in the audience, there were a few of them in attendance. Predictably, they caused a scene, shouting hateful nonsense that made no sense to anyone but other LaRouche-bots.

To be clear, I did not see the events that happened next, because people were quickly on their feet shouting the dummies down. But they were *right* by Al Franken, and the story in the hall was that it was Al Franken who hauled these petulant brats out with his own two hands, to the raucous cheers of the crowd. Imagine being so small and weak that *Al Franken* takes two of you on and wins. Anyway, it always made me doubly sad about the way things went down with Al.

You'd think that would be the unlikeliest thing I saw in New Hampshire. It was not. One of the things you don't realize is just how many people run for president that you'll never otherwise hear of. I guess this is especially true in New Hampshire, where presidential politics is entertainment for a lot of people. In addition to the winners and the big-name also-rans, there is a crowd of candidates who are running for absolutely no discernable reason. People like Caroline Killeen, who received eleven votes in the 2008 Democratic Primary, or H. Neil Fielding Jr., who received thirteen votes in the Republican primary the same year. Or Donald Trump.

I came across the strangest also-ran imaginable.

The New Hampshire presidential primary became a personal tradition for me. On a 2008 visit I saw a small crowd of media and passersby gathered in a semicircle, again in downtown Manchester. Thinking this might be a chance to meet one of the big-name-but-not-going-to-win candidates, I walked over to see what was up. In the center of the circle was a man wearing a trench coat. His eyes were almost cartoonish; you could practically see them swirling in a mad rapture at the attention. But it was the giant vinyl boot, upside down on his head, that really took the cake. Spittle flecked his long gray beard as he held forth on time travel, passing laws forcing people to brush their teeth, and general anarchy. His name was Vermin Supreme, and he won forty-one votes—which was more than John Cox, the Republican who lost to Gavin Newsom in the California governor's race, received a decade later.

Vermin. Supreme.

At least Vermin Supreme didn't upstage me. But the vote goat did.

Back in 2017, Rob Quist was running in a special election against Greg Gianforte for governor of Montana. Gianforte is a GOP bully who literally body-slammed a reporter on the eve of that election and somehow still won. But before that happened, Rob asked me to come to Montana and help get out the vote on college campuses. I *love* the face-to-face, and I love getting young people participating in the process, so it was easy for me to say yes to this. I flew to Montana and spent a few days visiting colleges around the state. I was going to help people register for absentee ballots, make sure they knew where to vote, and even drive some students to election offices to make sure everything was in order.

But nobody told me about the goat.

It was a baaaad time. There is nothing more demoralizing than knocking on a door, looking a student in the face, and seeing no recognition at all, but then having them universally squeal with delight at the goat visit. Apparently this goat had become an unofficial mascot of the Quist campaign, and I was now its sidekick. I got some kind greetings and some "Oh cool, my mom loves you." The goat got pets and hugs and selfies and the true red-carpet experience. And then, they just left me with the goat!

I know a lot of things. But I do not know how to take care of a goat, nor do I know my way around Montana.

So that is how I found myself in the middle of a college campus, with a goat happily munching on the grass under the lavish attention of young voters, while an election slowly slipped away.

But mostly, the campaign trail is an amazing place. Every year, at least before the pandemic, I made it a point to go to a state where there was a close election, rent a big van, and drive voters to the polls. Sometimes it was college students, sometimes it was seniors, and sometimes it was just people who didn't have another way to get out and vote. I've met amazing people and had deep and powerful conversations about the challenges they face—the challenges they hope to fix by voting. You're damn right I showed up in Alabama to bring people out to vote for Doug Jones and against Roy Moore. And it gave me such hope and inspiration to spend this time participating in the most important civic responsibility Americans have.

Campaigns aren't about the candidates, at the end of the day. Sure, that's where the focus is, and that's whose name ends up on the ballot. But campaigns are about the voters. They are about the lives of the people choosing leaders. They are a way of expressing ideas, and showing and understanding our differences with others, about how the people can best be served. It's worth remembering that elected officials are *public servants*. They are not monarchs. They are not deities. They are not above us.

And so this time and attention I've spent campaigning over the years has shifted my perspective away from the candidates and toward the people. The best campaigns don't start out by telling people what they are going to do; they start out by asking people what they need and then making plans to address those needs. It's why I'm a Democrat—take away the rancor and the personal enmity and the division of the twenty-first century, and look at the ideas: Democrats start with the idea that people come first. Republicans start with the idea that businesses come first. I'll always campaign for the people.

But keep your damn goats at home.

# Progressive or Performer?

The 2010s and early 2020s have been a time of rapid social change. The great thing about this is that we've seen a rise in people willing to dig in and do the work of allyship. This includes lots of listening, lots of self-examination, and lots of getting out of the way in support of people who have for too long had nowhere near enough support. But it's also created an opportunity for a number of people to enter the activism space with the intent of self-promotion, desperate for recognition and in a perpetual state of performative "wokeness." It's toxic, it's bad for activism, and it's ultimately counterproductive.

I've seen it happen over and over again during the "resistance" years, starting with the Trump campaign and really kicking into gear with his election. Somebody posts something that may be controversial or not exactly consistent with the loudest voices on one side or the other. Someone from another camp goes to town on them, in a ridiculous effort to demonstrate "wokeness." Want to know how to tell these people are full of shit? It's pretty easy: When people start an argument in public, invite them to have that same conversation in private. If they won't, they're performing for an audience instead of trying to have a conversation and change a mind. They're not interested in progress.

Performative activism is not about progress, it's about self-aggrandizement. People want to show they are on the right side, and rather than work toward changing hearts and minds, they work to demonstrate their own intelligence, or humor, or certainty that they have it all figured out. Often, when they do this, they deepen divisions and make it harder for the causes they claim to support to thrive in the world, but at least they've shown how correct they are. Over and over again, they call people out, often screaming at people who believe *almost the same things they do* over word choice, impeding what could otherwise be meaningful progress. It's often infuriating, always frustrating, and wildly counterproductive. It's also incredibly predictable and speaks to the reward system in the brain, as I've learned.

If you're Gen X or older, you remember those "This is your brain on drugs" commercials, where an egg sizzles away in a frying pan. Well, if your brain on drugs is a fried egg, your brain on dopamine is a unicorn flying through the bright sun.

It's evolution's way of keeping you doing the good things: giving you a reward for them. So when you get praise, or get validation, or have an orgasm, or eat something full of salt and fat, your brain shoots out dopamine so you keep doing more of whatever it was that you were doing. It's the exact opposite of pain, which is part of a punishment loop warning you off of doing the bad things.

But some people who employ performative actions, who show off instead of showing up, get that sweet, sweet dopamine release from demonstrating to the world just how woke they are. This neurotransmitter tells them that when the audience is watching them, it doesn't matter if they *do* the right thing, it matters that they *demonstrate* what they believe is the most right thing. This is where they've gone wrong. They've retrained their brain's reward system to release a dopamine flood when they flaunt their ideals instead of living them.

So, for example, when a white person says, "Black women believe . . . ," in an effort to shut down a discussion on voting rights, they've taken it upon themselves to be the spokesperson for Black women. I mean, this is the exact opposite of wokeness, but the reward system of this person's brain doesn't care. It's just pumping out dopamine as likes and retweets flood in from other white people performing their own little show. It's a feedback loop that shuts down the voices of those for whom they claim to speak, while lighting up their own brain. When it comes to dopamine rushes, performative wokeness and heroin addiction look a lot alike from a brain chemistry standpoint.

None of this is to say that there isn't a place to specifically call out bad behaviors and willful racism. When the president of the United States or other elected officials are enacting racist policies, you bet it's time to shout them out. But when Uncle Fred says that "the transgenders" deserve equal rights, maybe instead of getting our dopamine high by shouting at Uncle Fred on Facebook that "the transgenders" is not how one should talk about trans people, we need to retrain our brains instead. I mean, Uncle Fred wants to do the right thing, he wants to say the right thing, but he hasn't learned the right terms, the right language, and the right things to say.

When was the last time you learned anything by being shouted at? When we yell at old Uncle Fred, what he hears is that he can't please anybody and he's better off keeping his mouth shut. He's turned from an aspiring ally to someone who wants to sit on the sideline. He's been called out and publicly shamed for trying to do the right thing, and it's kept him out of the fight and probably resentful about it. That's a loss no matter how you look at it. But the person who called him out is probably smugly sitting in the glow of their screwed-up reward center, feeling proud of themselves for showing how good an ally they are instead of actually being a good ally.

Here's where dopamine should come in: when that person sends Uncle Fred a private message, or even better, gives him a call. "Hey, Uncle Fred! Saw that you were out there fighting for trans rights. That's amazing, so glad to see you taking a stand. Hey, one thing you might not know, and that I didn't know until somebody told me, is that instead of using 'the transgenders,' people prefer the term 'trans people.' Next time, give that a try—I think people will really appreciate it. And I'm here to help if you need me!" In this scenario, Uncle Fred feels seen, he feels helped, he feels advised, and he feels empowered to continue to make public statements in support of equal rights. We called him in instead of calling him out.

*That* should set off a dopamine rush, and a deserved one.

The root word of *progressive* is *progress*. If we're not making progress, not working toward progress, we're not progressive. It's why I met with Ted Cruz to talk about guns. Now, here's something interesting about that conversation—the senator and his team were supposed to meet with me and my team privately. But when we got there, he had it set up to livestream via his social media. He didn't want to have the private conversation; he wanted to display the public conversation. We still had the meeting, but I wonder how much easier it would have been to get down to brass tacks if the cameras were off and he didn't have an audience and the media to perform for.

I wonder if we would have made progress.

Van Jones made progress. And he did it by connecting with Donald Trump. Van is a man with a decades-long history of being an effective progressive activist. He's got a huge list of credentials in fighting for the environment, racial justice, and economic justice. He worked for the Obama White House. He's founded and led progressive organizations that do amazing on-the-ground work that has moved the needle forward. He is an arc bender, leading us to justice. And when he saw an opportunity to help people—mostly Black and brown people who were unjustly oversentenced—he didn't give a damn about political parties. He gave a damn about the people. Take, for example, Van's work on reducing jail terms for people who were incarcerated under mandatory-minimum drug sentences. His support of the FIRST STEP Act very likely made it possible to pass it, and when it was signed into law by Donald Trump, it reduced sentences for thousands of people. So-called progressives had been trying to get this done for years but demanded ideological purity in the bill and failed. They achieved nothing.

Van made progress, and the performers couldn't abide it. They couldn't take that he had possibly given a win to Trump, and they were willing to sacrifice the thousands of people the act helped to their own dopamine gods. A digital army of mostly white people spent weeks and months tearing Van down, a Black man with progressive cred that dates back longer than many of them have been alive, instead of celebrating the actual good this act did in the lives of so many people who had been treated unfairly. And they did it in public, making sure everyone saw just how "progressive" they were, as they attacked the agent of progress.

But they got their dopamine fix.

This is why we lose. It's why we lose over and over again, as the right snickers behind their hands and racks up footage to use against us in campaign ads. They cackle as we attack our own successes because we need to be *right* more than we need to be *effective*. They use it against us, highlighting the inanity of those who need the spotlight on themselves and painting the entire left with the folly of these bad actors. And while they are doing that, we're making Uncle Fred feel like he needs to just sit down and shut up, and maybe even vote for the other side, since they wouldn't give him such a hard time about not knowing the right word to use or when to use it.

I'm an actor. I'm no stranger to performing. But I work hard to never perform in my activism. If by meeting with Trump I could have done half of what Van accomplished, I would have done it in a heartbeat. If by meeting with Ted Cruz I can push any of the important gun violence prevention bills languishing in the Senate to the floor for a vote, I will take that meeting every time. I will—and I do, all the time—meet in private with elected officials from both parties, and most of those meetings I don't talk about at all in public. I'll meet in public if that's the only way they will do it. But I'll never do it for the sake of showing how progressive I am. I'll do it for the sake of progress.

I'm willing to set aside purity tests for the greater good. Every single person who calls themselves a progressive should too. And if they're not—they're no progressive. They're just a washed-up actor.

# By Any Other Name

There once was a rose in my life that I loved particularly strongly. This rose took so much effort to tend, but for a time I thought the beauty she exuded made the frequent prick of her hidden and vicious thorns worth the work. I was wrong.

Recently, I spent a weekend in my home in Tahoe, carefully arranging and planting a cascade of colorful flowers in my yard. Explosions of peonies and tulips in brilliant yellows and warm pinks sit alongside towering sunflowers and delicate lady's slippers. It's a restful, restorative place for me, where I can sit in the sun, take in the tall lodgepole pines in the distance, and breathe the sweet scents of my flower garden in the afternoon sun.

Roses used to be my favorite flower, but I no longer grow them. I've been pricked too many times. Roses are the most traitorous flowers—the demanding ones, so beautiful that you put in special effort to make sure the soil and water and air are just right. You spend hours digging a deep hole, for roses are picky flowers and do not like wet roots. You find the place in the yard that is best for the bushes, not best for your design. Roses need to be in the bright sunlight, anyone else's plans be damned. When they are not in the sunlight, they wither and wilt, drooping moodily for everyone to see.

Once the rosebush is planted, the hard work truly begins. You have to give it just the right amount of water or it will not thrive. Just the right amount of tending—too much, and its thorns will bite hard and deep and often; too little, and only the thorns will thrive. So you spend what is the right amount of time for the very special flowers, nurturing them, clearing choking vines from their path, making sure they have room to grow and breathe. You plant other flowers close enough so that the rose will still outshine them, but not so close that they have to interact in any meaningful way.

And still, one day when you have done all of the right things and the sun is out and you are sitting with your flowers and admiring them, a thorn will prick you. Small and hard and sharp, it will come for you when you are not expecting it. Perhaps you were simply tending to a nearby flower, and it jealously stabbed you as you walked past. Roses don't like it when other flowers get attention. Maybe someone was right in the middle of complimenting you on how hard you've worked on your garden, and people were starting to take notice. Roses don't like it when other people get credit for their work. Maybe it was just a cloudy day and the rose was bored, entertained by your pain.

Roses are vindictive.

The last time I paid attention to a rose, I was working with the women in my neighborhood to clear out a thicket of poison ivy that was threatening to overwhelm a wild rosebush down the street. This ivy was everywhere, choking out not only the roses but a whole hillside of wildflowers. But the roses were suffering the most, and so we started there. A number of us had suffered from the poison ivy's touch, and we could empathize with the rose. Together, we pulled the ivy up by its roots, exposing them to the bright sunlight that would kill the plant. We risked its retribution, knowing that just on the other side of our gloves toxic oils were oozing, waiting for one mistake to seep in and infect us—but together we stood strong. We cleared a ring around that rosebush, tending the soil, pruning back its tough, overgrown leaves so that its flowers could thrive.

We gave it space and attention at the same time, a truly impossible feat.

And still it thrust its thorns into my back as we packed up our gear to walk away. Dozens of thorns seemingly leapt from hidden stems when I wasn't looking. I yelped and hopped away from the bush. "Et tu, rose?" I thought through the pain.

I bled crimson into my work shirt and felt the sting immediately. I was reminded of how toxic roses could be: The first person to be treated with penicillin was Constable Albert Alexander, a British police officer who had been scratched by a rose in 1941, much like I had been too many times to count. Back then, our medicines were not powerful enough, and Constable Alexander died. I could feel the toxicity seeping into my skin from the cut, and I wondered how badly I had been poisoned. But our medicines are stronger now, and I, having been scratched and pricked and attacked by roses and tougher plants, have developed a degree of immunity.

And so I went home and stepped into a hot shower to wash the drying blood from my skin, the parade of punctures up my back stinging in the soap. My husband slathered the wounds with antibiotic ointment and helped me cover them with loose bandages. Every day, my children would ask how I was feeling, and the concern and love in their voices healed me more than any medicine. The community that helped clear out the poison ivy around the rose continued to work, clearing the weeds from the entire hillside. Soon, every flower there was strong and bright, their combined beauty drawing the eye away from the spiteful and jealous rosebush on which we had spent so much time.

The skin on my back quickly healed, and within weeks, the last vestiges of the hurt that had been done to me had been erased. No longer did I feel the scabs pull tight when I went to tend the other flowers. No longer did I need help applying ointments to the cuts. They were gone.

Some of my friends, some of the people I love best, said I should go and pull that rosebush up by its roots. "This rosebush is a lie," they said. "It looks beautiful, but it's dangerous. Inside, it's poison." But I never wanted to pull up the rosebush. I worked hard to save it. I would work hard to save it again—it's beautiful, and it had been so threatened by the poison ivy for so long that it didn't know any other way to act. I didn't want it torn up. I wanted to see it thrive, to find happiness in its place. To feel the sun on its petals, to see the beauty of the nearby wildflowers, and to be able to celebrate it all.

But I still don't grow roses. I don't keep them near me. I remember the cut of the thorns in my back. I remember the bright blood on my shirt and the care and concern in the eyes of my family. I remember the penicillin policeman, dying from the thorn. And I know that at least some roses are too toxic, too wild, to keep in my yard.

I still love them, though. Every once in a while, I'll drive by that rosebush and stop to admire it. Part of me wants to go to it. To let it know I forgive it—that it can't control what it learned to be. And to continue to help pull the weeds up when they creep into the clearing we built around the bush. But every time I take that step, the thorns flash menacingly under the dry and brittle leaves. Some bushes are so toxic that they need to be pulled up by the roots. And so, finally, I dig as the blood pours from my finger on the last visit, pulling the roots and giving the culture of that wild garden a reboot. Sadly, I walk back to the car, start it up, and come home to my own garden, where the flowers are fresh and beautiful and ready to thrive without hurting anyone else.

# The Lost Art

On August 21, 1858, Illinois Democrat Stephen Douglas and Illinois Republican Abraham Lincoln took the stage on a hot afternoon before a crowd of more than ten thousand people. It was the first of what would be seven such debates as each man tried to gain control of the state legislature for their party, which at the time was the body that elected senators. Now locked in history as the Lincoln-Douglas debates, what happened was unimaginable today, and that's a truly sad thing.

The last time these two men had met publicly (minus some speeches they'd given just before the debates that same year) was in 1854, when Lincoln absolutely crushed Douglas in his now-famous Peoria speech. If you read that speech—and you really should—you hear Lincoln say something radical for the time: "my ancient faith teaches me that 'all men are created equal'; and that there can be no moral right in connection with one man's making a slave of another." This speech was written in response to Douglas's Kansas-Nebraska Act, which allowed new states being admitted to the Union to decide whether they would be slave states or free states no matter whether they were Northern or Southern, and was effectively the precursor to the Civil War.

Historian Mark Neely's *The Abraham Lincoln Encyclopedia* (Da Capo Press, 1982) sets the scene: First, Stephen Douglas took the stage. For sixty minutes, he hammered at Lincoln on the issue of slavery, portraying him as an antislavery radical who wanted to "abolitionize" Illinois. While his ideas are abhorrent, especially by today's standards, he stood and spoke for sixty minutes on a hot summer afternoon on ideas of identity and politics while a giant crowd, nearly all of them standing, listened. And if that wasn't remarkable enough, Lincoln then responded for *ninety* minutes, defending himself from those allegations—although at heart he truly was such an abolitionist, as his Peoria speech demonstrated. Still, the crowd stood rapt, watching these two candidates expound on ideas and history.

Then, when Lincoln, his high and far-carrying voice tiring from the duration of his speech, finally ended his oratory, Douglas rebutted for *another* thirty minutes.

If we still did this, if debate still meant what it meant then,

Donald Trump would never have become president. We never would have found our nation in the dire straits the last half of the 2010s brought us. We often call debate a lost art, and it's true. But watching debate, learning from debate, demanding our leaders be able to expound on their ideas for hours, knowing them in depth and nuance and context? That's the lost art that matters.

I think back on the 2020 Democratic primary "debates," and I can't do anything but cringe. I mean, I loved the candidates—almost all of them. They were smart and bold and visionary and had lots of interesting things to say. But there were twenty of them, and we crammed ten of them on a stage at once, gave them only two hours to split between them, and pretended they provided a night of substance. These ten people, each vying to be not a senator of a single state but the president of the entire nation, received an hour less to split between ten people than Lincoln and Douglas used for just two.

It's a farce.

It's easy to blame social media, and the cable news cycle, and the busier lives we lead in a mass-media age. It's even correct to blame them. I remember the first CNN debate of the 2020 season, way back in the summer of 2019. It was announced like WrestleMania, hyping up divisions in the party

in a preposterous parody of credibility. LET'S GET READY
TO CRUMBLE!

These shows were not information, they were entertainment, served in bite-sized portions for a social-media-friendly
blitz after the fact. Almost nothing of substance happened or
was discussed in any way—and how could it have been? In
the first two-night, no-holds-barred cage match, each candidate averaged only eight minutes of speaking time. Eight.
Minutes. Or less than 10 percent of the time Lincoln and
Douglas took to air out their respective positions. It meant
that nobody was trying to win on the ideas, they were trying to win on the viral moments. These debates were bad for
the candidates, bad for the Democratic Party, and bad for
America.

But the reason they were allowed to go on that long, the
reason they happened that way, is because they were *giving us
what we want.* We are to blame for how far we've fallen. We've
allowed ourselves to become susceptible to the lowest common denominator of public discourse, tuning out nuance and
living by what drives trends. Can you imagine if we asked
Donald Trump, in the 2016 Republican debates, to go on at
length about how big his . . . hands were? I assure you, there
would be no length to that discussion.

But that's it—here, years in the future, that's what we

remember from that series of GOP debates in 2016, which were even worse than their 2020 Democratic counterparts. Donald Trump won because of those debates, not because he said anything of substance. That man never in his life uttered a substantial sentence that didn't end with "and I want fries with that." He won it because he said such outlandish, vile, hateful, wild things that the news cycle we demanded was breathless with his name. Every debate it was "What will Trump do next? Whose family will he insult? How low will he go?" People gave this man who called himself a billionaire hundreds of millions of dollars just to see what he would do. It was a juggernaut of jiggling junk, and we couldn't turn off our televisions.

We got what we deserved. We lost control of the monster we created in our decades-long confusion of news with entertainment. At its heart, this was no different than the paparazzi sneaking private beach photos of royals or celebrities, but instead of justifiable personal embarrassment, the consequences were measured in hundreds of thousands of lives and the near demise of our own democracy. We created it when we kept buying the paparazzi photos, and when we kept expecting our news to titillate us instead of educate and inform us.

Can you imagine what those 2016 Republican debates

would have looked like if Mr. Lincoln, a former member of Congress from Illinois, had been on that stage?

BRET BAIER, Fox News: Mr. Lincoln, Mr. Trump has called you soft on immigration for your position on emancipation. How long have you been willing to allow an invasion of the Northern states, sir?

MR. LINCOLN: It's a truth that I, born of strong faith and endowed by my Creator, have found the abolition of slavery to be an issue that is both morally and spiritually—

MR. TRUMP: He's weak, Bret. These people, they're just coming. Criminals. Swarming the border. And he's just going to let them in.

MR. LINCOLN: As Mr. Trump is aware, we and the other gentlemen, gathered here in the spirit of thinking and acting anew, have placed upon ourselves some boundaries of decorum and time, so that each in his turn may—

MR. TRUMP (in a mocking, high-pitched voice): Oh no, Mr. Trump is breaking the rules. Oooohhh noooooo.

BRET BAIER: I'll allow it.

SEN. CRUZ: Now, on this, I agree with Donald.

MR. TRUMP: I know your father was a murderer, ugly Ted. Get a load of this guy's wife. She's the unluckiest woman in America, having this guy's kids. And they all hate him! Everybody hates Ted. Many people say he's the most hated man in history. I don't know. I don't know, folks.

Sᴇɴ. Cʀᴜᴢ (crying): Donald, I know you only hurt the people you love.

Mʀ. Lɪɴᴄᴏʟɴ: Now, I do believe the time, though it passes faster than it passed last year, and the year before that, and so on, still belongs to me by the rules binding this event and drawing these good people together to hear what we have to say. Before proceeding, let me say I think I have no prejudice against the Southern people. They are just what we would be in their situation. If slavery did not now exist among them, they would not introduce it. But on the issue of emancipation—

Mʀ. Tʀᴜᴍᴘ: Now he's just making up words. Man-pants-nation? Get a load of this guy [*makes obscene gesture*]. Okay, Mr. Man Pants. We're waiting to hear why you're for letting hordes of criminals swarm the North and bother the good people. He just lost the plantation owners.

(APPLAUSE from GOV. WALKER, GOV. HUCKABEE, and BRET BAIER)

Sᴇɴ. Cʀᴜᴢ: Donald Trump is so great, I'd even try to over-throw a government to keep him in power. Just you wait.

The scary thing is, that's probably not too far from how it would have gone, and we would have still had Donald Trump as president even with a mind of the caliber of Lincoln's on the stage. So what does that say about us? What does it mean that when given the worst option—the very worst possible option—we'll elect it if it's entertaining? Why can't we find our way past this broken system and engage in ideas and nuance and detail in the way we need to if we want to address the dire issues of our time?

The first place we need to begin this work is in schools. Now, I don't want anyone to think I'm blaming teachers here—I'm not. What teachers do is superhuman. But too often, the curricula from which they have to work rely on teaching facts but not necessarily applying them to the present. We fail not only our kids but also our entire society when we fail to teach a rich tapestry of civics from a very young age. In 2018, when I was working to keep Brett Kavanaugh off of the Supreme Court, a C-SPAN poll came out showing that more than half of Americans couldn't even name a single Supreme Court justice. It's heartbreaking. Participation in and understanding of our political system needs to be seen as one of our most sacred responsibilities. Kids need to understand that if they can be expected to sit through a math lesson, or a baseball game, or anything else at all that takes attention and focus over an extended period of time, it's even more important to spend a similar amount of time invested in our government. If we miss a baseball game, we might be bummed out. If we miss an election, we fail to exercise the most important right we possess and shirk the responsibility we have to one another: steering the direction of our nation.

More people did not vote in 2016 than voted for any presidential candidate. The biggest vote getter was "no vote at all." This changed a little bit in 2020: Joe Biden got more votes than "did not vote," but Donald Trump did not, as eighty million eligible voters didn't cast a ballot. And I know some of you are sitting there and saying, "Yeah, well, the candidates were terrible." Well, I disagree on one side at least, but if that's what you think, there is a cure! Participate in the process. That's the only way to shape the political system. When one-third of Americans give us a president, two-thirds of Americans are left out every single time. It's what the entrenched powers know—and at least one side counts on. When Mitch McConnell figured out so few people were paying attention, he stopped doing his job and let America break to its very core. He made the entirety of his job about preventing progress: He called himself the "grim reaper" and did not move forward on hundreds of bills that passed the House—many with bipartisan majority votes—during his tenure as Senate majority leader.

But it's not just teachers: Parents, neighbors, grandparents, you have to bring this responsibility into your homes. You have to instill the value of participatory democracy, the values that the early American revolutionaries fought to instill, no matter how flawed they were, as part of your household. Spend time at dinner talking about a political issue. Take your kids with you when you vote. Go to town meetings, run for select boards, be part of the civil processes of your town. Build a generation of Americans, not just people who live in America.

Maybe it's time to let younger people vote. Maybe it's time for sixteen-year-olds who pass a civics curriculum focused on the voting process, identifying disinformation, and participating in community service, including volunteering at polling places, to have a say in what happens in their future. How transformational would that be for our country? How cool would it be to get kids invested in their own civics education and reward them for success with a voice? When we give people a reason to be part of the system and a sense of earning the full rights of citizenship, the responsibilities that come with that citizenship will mean so much more.

And then, maybe, when a presidential candidate spends time on the debate stage talking about the size of his penis, we'll show him the size of our education. We can demand more of our leaders when we are paying attention to their substance instead of their showmanship. We can earn back the Lincoln-Douglas debates and take our places as citizen-leaders. It's the essence of being an American.

# Milo

Holy shit, giving birth sucked. I know women are supposed to talk about how magical and empowering the experience was, how it defined motherhood and sacrifice and connection to their babies. But no. I will not pretend I enjoyed it. It fucking hurt. I was torn, and bled, and nothing went to plan. Years later I still have a fissure from postlabor constipation. It was not magic, it was *work*, and it was pain.

I mean, it was worth it. But it was the worst.

The day Milo was born was sultry, with shimmers of heat coming off the pavement as I left a prenatal yoga class. Now, if you looked at Instagram, you'd think yoga was relaxing, with perfectly made-up women smiling gracefully over their sports bras and Lululemons while contorting into poses that nobody was ever meant to attain. But that's because I did not put my pregnancy yoga photos on Instagram. Week by week it became more hilarious as I tried to work around my growing belly, getting sweatier and grumpier and much less made up as my pregnancy went on. Normally around 120 pounds, I had ballooned to a round 170. I had gained fifty pounds, but I didn't even know it—I refused to look at the scale during my maternity checkups.

If you've ever doubted the elasticity of yoga pants, just know I never changed my size during my entire pregnancy.

Anyway, since I was birthing his child, my husband decided to take the last few days of my pregnancy off. He picked me up from yoga and took me straight to my favorite sub place. Sitting outside in the heat, I ate the hell out of a turkey sandwich, mayo dripping out the far end and pickles piled higher than was advisable over the meat. Pregnant women loving pickles is a stereotype for a reason, after all. David had some kind of processed meat, and we talked about nothing. We didn't hold hands and gaze into one another's eyes as we imagined our baby's arrival together. I didn't know it was the last meal we'd have as a childless couple.

And so we went home. I warmed up a pretzel in the microwave, stole my favorite blanket back from my thieving dog, and snuggled in for an afternoon nap. As I lay down, I felt the mattress squish beneath me in a way I had never felt as a lighter woman. It was a good nap—I mean, all naps are good, but this one was just right. When I woke it was late in the day, and when I struggled to get out of bed I felt a trickle of warm liquid run down my thigh. It was ten days before my due date, so I didn't think it was my water breaking—as compacted as my bladder was by my very full womb, it was not impossible that it was a little bit of pee—but I texted my ob-gyn just to be safe, and she asked me to come in.

I mean, I had always imagined that when my water broke, it would be a big SPLOOSH of liquid pouring out of me. I was sure I would be sure. Hell, my birthing coach recommended carrying around a jar of pickles in the grocery store to drop and break in case my water broke in the aisles and I didn't want anyone to know. I thought it would be a lot. And this was just a trickle.

Well, guess what? Yup, it was amniotic fluid. I had a small tear in my amniotic sac, and the fluid was slowly leaking. My ob-gyn told me to go home, take a shower, put on some makeup, and get myself checked into the hospital. And so I did.

I'm a bit of a control freak. I'm also a planner, and so I had this measured out to the very smallest detail. I'm pretty sure David threw his back out maneuvering my very, very full hospital bag into the car. It was so big, he was probably relieved when he was just helping my 170-pound frame into the front seat.

I wasn't having any contractions at this point and still felt great. We called my family and my closest friends to let them know what was happening, and we were on our way. Everything was going to plan, and that plan was VAGINAL BIRTH OR BUST. I had spent nine months hitting every single birthing class I could find. I had taken special classes just on breathing during labor. On breastfeeding. On getting your baby to sleep. I had read every book it was possible to read. I knew exactly what to expect when I was expecting.

You know that saying that man plans and God laughs? Well, when a woman plans, God *cackles*. Nothing could have prepared me for the actual experience. I was wheeled into the hospital at seven P.M. with fresh mascara and a smile and put on the gown they gave me. David started pulling out the birthing tools and marking them off on the checklist I had prepared for him:

Digital frame, check. We had programmed it to scroll photos of the family and my five dogs and nine horses. Together, we had decided this would be a good focal point for when things got stressful.

iPod and speakers, check. We had a special playlist just for this occasion filled with songs we both loved, including a lot of nineties hip-hop. I didn't need an epidural; I had "Gin and Juice."

Birthing ball, check. I still don't think David knows what that is, but God bless him, he packed it.

My favorite pillow, check.

A mirror so I could watch the birth, check.

Two cameras, just in case, check.

Phones, chargers, deodorant, lotions, check, check, check, check.

I'm sure the nurses still tell stories about the crazy Bugliaris, who showed up with seven babies' worth of supplies.

And nothing happened. We were settled in, I was in a gown surrounded by stuff, and I was bored out of my wits. No contractions, no pain, no need to breathe, nothing. It was just me and David and a gown that showed the world my butt.

Finally, after about two hours, my doctor waltzed in.

"Well," she said, "with tears like this the biggest risk is that it exposes the baby to bacteria and he can get an infection. So we're just going to induce and get this whole thing started."

Not. Part. Of. The. Plan.

"Rupturing the sac at nine P.M." was *not* on David's checklist. Milo wasn't even born yet and he was teaching me about parenting. "Oh really, Mom? You had a plan? Okay, boomer." I'm still trying to learn to be flexible in my parenting, and this was my first lesson. It's so hard for a control freak to let this go.

I remember the nurse hooking me up to a fetal monitor and starting an IV to get the Pitocin going. This is a medicine that starts contractions and induces labor.

"This wasn't the plan," I told her.

"Oh, honey," she said with a smile. "You'll get used to that." And then the drip was running and the doctor came in with a medieval torture implement. It looked like a long, evil crochet hook. I swear she was grinning maniacally, but that could be my imagination. I shit you not, Neil Young was singing "The Needle and the Damage Done" on the iPod. It was surreal.

"What the hell is that for?" I asked.

"This is what I'm going to break your sac with. I will go in, latch on to a little section, and pop it."

I looked at that torture device in her hand, at my husband, and back at the doctor. I blinked a few times. I squeezed my knees tightly together. "You go in through my mouth, right? Please say that's how you get there."

That got a laugh. An evil laugh, I think.

And *that's* when my parents walked in the room. I didn't know if I was happy about that or not. I mean, I learned my controlling ways from my mom, and my dad was already crying. He looked at the monitor. "Is that his heartbeat?" he asked.

And that was the first time I noticed Milo's heartbeat was filling the room. My dad has a way of making everything better. He did so in this moment. Now I had something real to focus on, the steady, wet *whoosh* of his heartbeat. Oh, how I loved him already. I would've done anything to make sure he

was safe and healthy. Even get prodded by an enormous crochet needle.

One thing they don't teach in birthing classes is the most
invasive thing that exists on the planet happens when you
have a baby: EVERYBODY has access to your vagina. Doctors and nurses come on in and touch your cervix. People you
love are there with cameras to film the whole process. During
one of these checks, my brother and his girlfriend arrived.
Soon after, my best friend, Alaa, came in, bringing the smell
of smoke and scotch with him and making everyone laugh. It
was a party in my privates. I love my uncle Mitch to death, but
I am so glad he stayed in the waiting room.

This was a joyous group, and they were giddy and excited
to meet Milo and having a grand old time, and I was so happy
for it. But by around eleven P.M. the Pitocin was doing its
thing, and I was having some pretty serious contractions every five minutes. Each one was like being washed over by the
biggest, strongest wave you've ever seen, and right before I
drowned, it let up. I would start to catch my breath, climb out
of the wet sand, only to be clobbered by the next one. There
was no way to stay ahead of the pain.

A nurse checked my cervix. I was only four centimeters
dilated. Six. Fucking. Centimeters. Left.

"Oh my God," I told her. "I'm going to die."

"No," she said. "You're going to have a baby."

After the next contraction, and a string of language so foul that the MPAA gave my birthing movie an NC-17 rating, the nurse gently suggested I get an epidural to help manage the pain.

"No, no, no. That is not part of my birthing plan. I have a plan!" I gestured to the frame, currently displaying one of my dogs. I love my dogs so much, but everything still hurt.

She looked at me and said, "The sooner you learn to go with the flow, the easier everything will be for you."

I knew she was talking about more than the epidural. My whole life, I'd wanted to have babies. I was the little girl who would rather play with my baby cousin than friends my age. I would dream of breastfeeding, and holding a tiny little hand, and changing diapers, and late-night feedings. I wanted it all. But when I hit my thirties, I think my family kind of gave up hope that it would ever happen for me. I didn't want to have kids with the wrong man, and I hadn't met the right one. And then came David. My beautiful David.

The first time I met David's father, I knew what a great dad he would be. We got married in 2009 on the property he grew up on and started trying for a baby right after. The very first time we had sex after "pulling the goalie," I got pregnant.

And then, at the age of thirty-eight, I miscarried. I was completely crushed. Devastated. I remember going to the doctor and trying unsuccessfully to find a heartbeat. It felt like God was punishing me for the abortions I'd had in my twenties. As we sat in the parking lot of the medical building after that appointment sobbing and holding each other, he grabbed my face, looked into my eyes, and said, "It's okay. We're going to have another baby. A *better* baby. That baby was a Red Sox fan." And in that moment of some of the most desperate pain I have ever felt, I laughed.

Three months later we were pregnant with Milo.

"YES! GIVE ME THE DAMN EPIDURAL," I moaned.

When you're in pain, you want everything to happen quickly. Almost nothing happens quickly in a hospital unless someone is dying. By the time the anesthesiologist showed up to give me the epidural, I was ready to kill someone to get them to move quickly. I had also progressed from four to seven centimeters. After a burning deep in my spine from the epidural needle, the pain started to let up.

The rest is kind of a blur. I remember yelling at my mother for looking at me, and wondering if I was hallucinating when I opened my eyes to see Alaa, David, and my mother dancing to nineties rap. David was a DJ in college, so he even rapped along.

And then a nurse came in and told me it was time to push.

"But where's my doctor?" I think it was about three A.M. by this point.

"She's in bed sleeping. She told me to give her a call when you get close. Oops."

"Oh."

I saw David. He looked exhausted and murderous.

I really don't know what I thought pushing was going to be like. But I *do* know I didn't think it would involve a nurse up to her elbows in my vagina while manipulating a reticent baby to take the exit. I *also* didn't think David would take the term *birth coach* quite so literally. "C'mon, baby! You got this! Dig deep! Bear down!" I swear to God I thought he was about to start chanting "RU-DY! RU-DY!"

I pushed for three and a half hours.

Milo wouldn't come out.

I later learned that David carried a lot of guilt for pushing me so hard for so long. It wasn't his fault. We had a plan. The sun rose, and the room came into a sepia relief. I was more exhausted than I had ever been. And then my doctor waltzed in, looking fresh as a daisy.

"I could have told you this would happen. We can keep trying, but I'd recommend taking the cesarean at this point."

*We?*

I looked at David. He looked back at me.

"I'm so tired," I said. It had been eighteen hours since that little trickle started this trial. "Let's meet our baby."

And before I knew what was happening, I was on a cold table in a very, very bright room. The Pitocin in my IV was swapped out for something that made me very, very hazy. A glaring white light shined down into my tired eyes. It felt like judgment. I saw that my mom and David were in the room, wearing blue paper gowns, ridiculous blue hats, and masks. I felt no pain, just some pushing, and then some pulling. And then?

A cry. THE cry. The most joyous, wonderful sound I had ever heard. They put him on my chest. My perfect baby. My Milo.

He climbed and found my nose and suckled my happy, salty tears. Happy not only because he was finally here, but also so, so happy that it was over.

Or so I thought.

They teach you a lot of things, but not what happens. Not what is real. And not that the end of birth is just the very beginning of everything that matters.

They also didn't teach me that I wouldn't be able to shit for ten days. That would have been good to know.

I love being a parent, but man, do I hate giving birth.

# Words

Words are weird, right? I mean, they are a collection of sounds, represented by letters, to which we ascribe meanings and power. They are completely arbitrary—this collection of sounds means that small furry animal whose poop I clean up out of the backyard several times daily, while this other collection of sounds means "an orange dictator who can't stop overcompensating for small things by placing his name"—another collection of sounds and letters—"on all the buildings he defaults on." At some point in history, someone said, "This sound means this," and everyone eventually hopped on the bandwagon. But it is the power some words have over others—and the way we use that power—that baffles me.

When I look at the things my trolls say to me, incessantly, I usually laugh. It's such a weak collection of small men who are obviously terrified of women and the power that comes from being a woman. It's why they use the words that are tied to the identity of cisgender women as slurs. "You're a cunt," they say, over and over again.

"**Cunt** (kunt) *n* 1) the vulva or vagina; 2) sexual intercourse with a woman; 3*a*) a woman (a term of hostility and contempt) . . . 4) any unpleasant or contemptible person."[1]

Let that sink in.

It can mean a woman's genitals, a woman, or any truly terrible human. Who in the world comes up with this shit? Oh right. Men. Men come up with this. There is no way in hell that a cisgender woman, whose genitals can stretch so wide that a living being the size of a watermelon can just pop on out of them, decided that calling someone a cunt was an insult. And we see that throughout language. Men create words that use the differences between less powerful groups to belittle them. They attack the differences, as that is the only way they can keep their superiority ingrained in our culture. You want to call me a cunt? Great! Balance a watermelon on your dick for a year, and then come talk to me.

And it doesn't stop at *cunt*. The dizzying array of insults aimed specifically at cisgender women based on our biology is astounding. *Pussy. Twat. Minge. Vag. She's on the rag. Bitch.*

---

1   *Webster's New World College Dictionary*, 5th ed. (Boston: Houghton Mifflin Harcourt, 2018), 364.

Then they attack us for the same sexuality they celebrate in themselves. There is no male equivalent to *slut*.

"**Slut** (slut) *n* 1) a careless, dirty, slovenly woman; slattern; 2) a sexually promiscuous person, esp. a woman: a derogatory or insulting term."[2]

Go ahead and find a male equivalent of that. I'll wait.

Oppression starts in language, and language is one of the first things we learn as infants. Long before we have the ability to say specific words or phrases, we internalize the meanings, attitudes, and biases inherent in them. As children grow, both the usage and the words themselves become normalized. Right from the very start of our lives, we are fighting the oppression of the words we use; we are not born biased, but our language teaches bias from our earliest days. We see pink and soft and think "girl." We think "fragile." We think "delicate." And we think "less than."

My daughter, Bella, plays baseball. Not softball (but there's another one—girls play "softball." Have you ever been hit by a softball? Seen a softball pitch? Not a damn thing soft about it), which is what girls are so often relegated to, but baseball, *like her brother*. And her coach, who is a kind and well-meaning man, calls her "honey," while calling the boys "bud" or by their names. Honey is sweet. Honey is slow. Honey is not

---

2   *Webster's New World College Dictionary*, 1370.

tough. Honey is something you put in your tea, not your pitching rotation. This is what she learns from one of the first men to teach her together with a bunch of boys. He's not a bad man—he's a good man, kind and smart and caring—and does not want less for my daughter than I do. But he's been conditioned by language to treat her differently, and she is learning that conditioning. Worse, so are the boys on her baseball team.

Imagine the uproar if he called a boy on his team "honey." Imagine your own reaction to a grown man calling your daughter "honey" and the difference in that reaction if he called your boy "honey." There you'll see the biases revealed in language. Patriarchy. Homophobia. Other. *Less than*. Language is how we learn.

In my house, we don't have the normal "dirty words" that most other kids have. *Fuck*? How is the act of lovemaking dirty? *Shit*? It's a natural biological process. This is how weird language is: *poop* is *shit* for kids. It means the exact same thing—you can use them interchangeably in any single instance—but one has a power the other lacks. Neither of them are on the forbidden-words list in my house, although my kids know that other people probably feel differently about those words than David and I do.

No, the words we ban? *Stupid* and *dumb*.

I want to break this down a little bit, but before I do, I want

to point out that each of these words is often used as a modi-
fier for the gender-based slurs I already talked about. "You
dumb whore" is a favorite of those small, scared men yelling
at me on Twitter. So is "you dumb cunt." As if they can't con-
tain all of their smallness in the first word, they have to add to
it. Imagine being that weak little man-child, hiding away in
his "man cave" where he doesn't have to face his wife's contempt for how low he is, and not thinking *cunt*, the worst word
you can think of, is a strong enough word, so he adds *dumb* in
front of it. It would be funny if it weren't so harmful. Instead,
it's just sick.

Anyway, on to *stupid*.

"**Stupid** (stōō'pid) *adj* ... 2) lacking normal intelligence or
understanding; slow-witted; dull."[3]

This is where we get to the othering of people at a very fundamental level. Implied in *stupid* is a fundamental inequality,
a flaw in the *capacity* to reason. Stupidity cannot be overcome
with learning; it is different from ignorance or misunder-
standing. If somebody is stupid, that person is, and forever
will be, less than normal. This word, this concept, is powerful.
It connects with something inherent in a human, and hearing
from a young age that one is stupid will leave scars so thick, so

---

3   *Webster's New World College Dictionary*, 1442.

hard, and so ugly that nobody can ever be expected to over-come them.

When a child calls another child stupid, it lingers. It is a word with claws, deep and sharp hooks that set themselves in the tender self-image of too many kids. It is especially true for girls, who are already taught math and science differently than boys, who are *presumed* to be inherently less able to com-prehend and express STEM principles than boys are (see how closely linked this is with the idea of stupidity?). The results are devastating for our world and for our country. We know that many fewer girls grow up to be women in the sciences, and it starts with the idea of stupid. Imagine what diseases would be cured if we did not treat girls this way already. We could have solved the climate crisis, or cured all kinds of can-cer, or elected a president who didn't think nuking a hurri-cane was a terrific idea.

But we haven't. THAT is stupid.

And if you think *stupid* is bad, let's look at *dumb*.

"**Dumb** (dum) *adj* 1) lacking the power of speech; mute...; 6) lacking some normal part, characteristic, or quality; 7) ... stupid, moronic."[4]

My friend Ady Barkan is a lawyer. He's one of the smartest humans on the planet. And a terrible, debilitating disease has

4   *Webster's New World College Dictionary,* 451.

taken his voice from him. Is he less than? Is he "stupid" or "moronic" because ALS paralyzed his diaphragm and vocal cords? What about autistic children who are speech delayed, or those with other diseases? Kids who lose their voice to cancer? The idea that we are linking intelligence with the ability to vocalize and using that as a basis to diminish others is such a hateful, sickening concept that my stomach turns when I hear those words in my home.

Words like *stupid* and *dumb* erase potential. We took these sounds, filled them with hate, and used them to steal the future of those we fear. It is social propaganda, hurting whole swaths of people. We take away the very idea from individuals that their ideas matter, that they can make a difference, and we squash the confidence they need to see those ideas through. Ady Barkan is changing the world without speaking a word. Ady is not less than. He is more than, infinitely more than. And so are so many of those who speak or learn differently, who have unlimited potential right up until we put the limiters on.

Language is weird. But words have power.

Rejection hurts. It's sometimes necessary, but never in the actual structure of our language. I know that Stephen King, one of the most successful writers ever to take up pen and ink, allegedly had a stack of rejection slips so thick that the nail he used to hold them to the wall could no longer support their bulk. *Lord of the Flies* and *Catch-22* were both rejected twenty times or more. Inherent in being a writer is being a rejected writer. You can break through that rejection, but it's so much harder to do if the words themselves reject who you are and not just the work you do.

I try to be careful in the words I choose to use, and even so, I know the biases I learned flow through my words. I say *crazy* when I mean "really unexpected" or "hard to believe" or "unusual." I say, "Hey, guys," to a group of people. And yes, I say things are dumb, and my children take no small delight in correcting me when I slip. I'm imperfect and the product of the world in which I live. But I know if we all were more careful with the things we said, and the ideas behind the words, our world would be so much better, so much more fair, and so much more advanced.

Language is changing. It's striving to be more inclusive. *Folx, Mx., Latinx, BIPOC*—there's an ongoing stream of advancements meant to be inclusive that are empowering people who for so long have been disempowered by our very words. It's important for us to remember that advancing our language does not mean being only additive to it. We have to prune it, to take out the words that lessen us, that keep us from growing, just as much as we need to add the new words to express a more enlightened world. We need to erase the limits that the men who crafted language put on the people who use it. Our words are our voice, and how we choose to use both affects everyone who hears our words. Being mindful in those choices will help our language—and our culture— evolve past some of its shortcomings.

# Patriotism

*Our country is not the only thing to which we owe our allegiance.*
*It is also owed to justice and to humanity. Patriotism consists*
*not in waving the flag, but in striving that our country shall be*
*righteous as well as strong.*

—JAMES BRYCE, politician and member
of the British Parliament

One of the strangest things that happened after 9/11 was the veritable flood of American flags suddenly displayed everywhere you looked. Demonstrative patriotism became big business, as if seeing a flag waving on a porch or stuck to the bumper of a foreign car would really show those terrorists a thing or two. If a politician—and especially a president—was seen without an American flag pin on their lapel (for some reason, this maxim applied particularly to men), well, all hell would break loose.

But we did this at the exact same time we let the stupidly named USA PATRIOT Act pass. You know, the bill that allowed surveillance of the books we took out of the library, allowed police and other law enforcement institutions to run roughshod over the Constitution, and embodied dozens of anti-American principles. It allowed the FBI to spy on mosques as we looked sideways at anyone with brown skin. It let airport screeners take 3D images of our naked bodies, put people on "no-fly" lists without judicial processes, let the government demand phone records without a warrant by issuing a letter, and allowed extrajudicial killing, torture, and everything that was contrary to the American mythos in the name of patriotism and security. As a country, we hid behind our flags while becoming our worst selves, pretending that we were coming together as a nation when we were actually casting out anyone who wasn't white and conservative.

This is not patriotism. This monster of a law was not born out of love of country; it was born out of fear. It perpetuated that fear, codified it, made it part of the very fabric of our identity as Americans. But we put a flag on it, called it the PATRIOT Act, and dared anyone to dissent.

I dissented. So did many of us. We continue to.

It's easy to love the people in your life when they are getting it right. It can be hard to love them when they are going astray. When the people I love, really love—those I want as part of my life for the rest of my life—do things that send them down a path I don't recognize, the only course of action is to tell them. To try to show them where they are going wrong and work to steer them in the right direction. This isn't an act of contrarianism or control—it's an act of love. Saying to someone, "I love you too much to stay silent while you hurt yourself," or, even worse, "while you hurt someone else," is the hardest bedrock of love. It is the place where we can speak honestly, where we are *compelled* to speak honestly. It is where we find one another at our lowest points, and that expression of love can be a lantern in the darkness that lights the way out. I know people who love me who have risen to that calling of frank honesty have saved me at times when I didn't know I needed saving. And I love them all the more for it.

I often talk about my journey into activism as a love story. And activism is, at its very heart, a powerful expression of patriotism. And as with the people in our lives, it is *easy* to love your country when it gets things right. It's harder to love your country when it gets things wrong. But when you love something, you stick it out in the hard times. Sure, there is a breaking point. There is a line, a point of no return where either personal or national relationships can no longer be salvaged. But that is not where we are, and activism can be couple's therapy for the nation. It is stating your needs and working to strengthen and improve the relationship. It is helping America be its best self.

Patriotism is believing in the potential of America and working like hell to help our nation see that potential realized. But realizing potential takes work. It takes close attention, probing the sore spots, figuring out what's making them hurt, and then fixing them. Every activist I know is a patriot. I can't say the same for everyone who has a flag decal. As a song by the late John Prine goes, your flag decal won't get you into heaven anymore. And, if we're being honest, it never would have.

The Bible tells us that faith without works is dead. And while I have complicated feelings about the institutions of faith, I am a believer. I can't imagine a clearer illustration of faith without works than a flag decal on the back of a monstrous gas-guzzling SUV. When I see a giant Hummer with an American flag, I can't help but laugh at the person driving it. Here they are chanting "USA" while driving a car gulping down Middle Eastern and Venezuelan oil, and I can absolutely guarantee you they have a Facebook page that screams about socialism and Muslims. They are the absolute epitome of not caring about a damn thing except themselves and the people they think matter, and apathy is antithetical to patriotism. But they would call themselves patriots, every damn day.

Militias are made up of these people. Their existence is very literally an armed resistance against the nation. They are there to give the finger to the government, hiding behind too many guns. They will train on their barricaded land to fight against the military and police of the nation they claim to love. They plot to kidnap and assassinate duly elected officials because they have political disagreements with them. They show up at polling places, marching back and forth with guns nobody should have, like AR-15s and other assault weapons, to intimidate voters and keep them from voting. And when they go home, they think they are patriots. These are the people who continue to cheer the PATRIOT Act, too stupid to realize that even they—no, *especially* they—are now targets of it.

They are not patriots. They are traitors. They are cancers in our nation, feeding on the things that are good and growing more mutated, dangerous, deadly cells. They could very well be the death of us, driving such division and hatred—the fruits of the cowardice plant—that we reach the point of no return. Where the identity of America is so shredded, so unrecognizable, that it cannot be saved. Her organs of justice and freedom may shut down, starved of the nourishment they need. But there is a treatment: activism.

If the false patriots are cancer, activists are the immune boosters, the chemotherapy, the gene therapy. Through hard work, electing the right people, promoting the right causes, and getting the right laws enacted, they can change the DNA of a society. They can slow down or stop the progression of the illness, reduce the number of cells that are trying to spread their broken code, and give the country space and time and strength to heal.

At the heart of this cure, at the heart of the medicine, is

love. If you don't have love in your heart, you can't be an effective activist. Sure, you can fight, you can oppose, but if the source of your passion is the conflict, you'll have nothing left when you win. Winning is just part of the goal of activism. The real work is what comes after winning. Everything from that point on is details. It's making sure what you worked for is going the way you intended, and being self-aware, self-reflective, and egoless enough to admit when it isn't. It's a constant process of evaluating your mistakes and fixing them. It is tedious. It can be hurtful and boring. It can feel like it will never happen. But it is a labor of love, and it is the most important part of doing the work.

What's not the most important part of doing the work? Press releases and fundraising.

This is a part of the activism community that drives me absolutely mad. Across every single issue, there are interest groups who rush to get out the first press release when something happens and take credit for whatever caused it. Of course, each of these press releases is followed by a flurry of fundraising emails. Unfortunately, all too often these actions come from the biggest organizations, who swoop in at the last minute and either take credit for the work of local organizers or, worse, sabotage their work altogether. But this happens all the damn time. And even worse, it often happens at the expense of the communities the activist groups purport to be trying to save—especially when those local groups are led by people of color.

Patriotism and self-promotion are mutually exclusive. The first is inherently about something greater than yourself. The second? Nah.

The thing about patriotism is that true patriots, like real activists, may never live to see their dreams fulfilled. There were those who wanted to see a nation like the United States on this land long before it was founded. And there were those who were already here who did not. The latter did not live to see the purpose of their struggle fulfilled. The former are still fighting the battle to protect their culture and lands. Activism is the same. Activists have to be content with the fact that no matter how hard they fight and how good they are at their work, for many cancers we do not yet have a cure. That the work they do will be incremental, and suffer setbacks, and will continue long after they are gone in most cases.

Patriotism is never being content with the status quo. Activism is the expression of that discontent.

I love this country. I love the ideals that cling to her core despite the great failings of the (mostly) men who have led her. I am, through and through, more patriotic than the sum total of every scared little white man hiding behind his guns and chanting "U-S-A" while calling Democrats tyrants because we've asked them to have the basic decency to wear a mask.

And I will never be content when America can be better. I don't expect to see that fulfilled while I am alive, but I know my children, and your children, and their children will carry on when I am gone. I know that my love for country, and your love for country, carries on in them. I know we will not be defeated.

I am a patriot. And I will never stop striving until my country is as righteous as it is strong.

=

# Ruth

R uth Bader Ginsburg is dead.

By the time you're reading this, that will be old news. But as I write, it happened yesterday. The presence of her absence is overpowering. She was a monumental figure in my life, an inspiration for my activism, a model of clear-thinking justice, and a trailblazing feminist. I am gutted.

There's a famous conceit that's been around at least since ancient Greece: the *mind palace*. It's a memory device, made famous by Sherlock Holmes. The idea is that you build a house of many rooms in your mind, each one storing specific details of events, allowing your mind to recall minutiae clearly and see patterns that might otherwise be hidden. Well, I'm the first person to tell you I'm no Sherlock Holmes, but it's an exercise I like to undertake. I don't have the memory part down just yet, but it does help me see patterns and possibilities of what might be to come. Today, the house of my mind has two windows, each looking out at a different future. The best of times and the worst of times. I can see them both clearly, and it's possible that you already know which one we are taking. I envy you that, the clarity of distance, the surety of the path already taken. I know that right now, right in this moment, it is the unsurety that is terrifying.

I look out the window to my left.

## THE BEST OF TIMES

Liz opened the door to her dorm room just before Thanksgiving break of her senior year at Smith. Her roommate was already gone, and the small space smelled of fall in New England. Somehow the mixture of the bright leaves, now mostly fallen from their trees and carpeting the green spaces of campus, always seemed to carry with it a suggestion of cinnamon when the wind blew. She'd started calling herself "Liz" just after she left for college, a break from the "Beth" she'd always gone by. It was an homage to her hero Justice Warren, who'd retired on the day she was accepted to Smith.

Like the rooms of many young people, hers was decorated

in a surprising array of conflicting ideas and images. An anarchy pin adorned her backpack, placed on a shelf next to her *Blackpink Reunion Tour 2035* poster. Classic rock like Weezer filled the iRing Smartsystem pierced into the fourth hole in her left earlobe, but so did the newest pop from Hillary Swift, Taylor's thirteen-year-old daughter, whose blend of pop and punk had catapulted her to young fame just like her mother. It was a display dedicated to freedom, to figuring things out, to having found her own path.

A ding from her iRing reminded her that she had an appointment to check her implant when she got home. The breakthrough medication, developed in part by her professor of pharmacology at Smith, prevented both pregnancy and the overwhelming cramping she used to experience before it was prescribed. Within weeks of getting the implant, she had felt great—no more missed classes from the pain, and no more side effects from the pill. As far as she was concerned, it was a wonder drug, and it blew her mind that it almost hadn't been allowed to come to market.

Ten years ago, when the manufacturer first applied for market approval, a small study had shown that if a pregnant woman received the implant in the early days of her pregnancy, it would cause a spontaneous abortion. A number of Southern states—and Rhode Island, weirdly—had sued the FDA to prevent its approval, saying that the drug violated the

Tenth Amendment, which they claimed allowed the states to set regulations on how abortions were performed. Women around the country marched, rallied, and voted, but it was up to the courts. Ultimately, Justices Warren, Sotomayor, Kagan, and Whitmer held the line for the liberal bloc of the court, and in a separate and surprising vote, Chief Justice Roberts had sided with them before retiring.

*That* did not go over well with the right. In a bizarre publicity stunt, Texas governor Ted Cruz had filed a petition of secession and tried to make Texas a sovereign republic before being resoundingly defeated in 2030. He had some radio show now and was talking about running for president with Joe Rogan. But nobody was really listening.

She also had an interview with GenesysAstra, the biggest American company in ethical pharmaceuticals. It was a big deal for her; they had an all-woman board, had a deep recruitment network at Smith, and had almost closed the pay gap in their company—and would have if not for a couple of tenured founders who refused to quit the company. Liz had good but not great grades, but she had an impressive résumé that included internships at some really prestigious firms and had served on the front lines in Burma, the latest bubble-up of the American-Chinese proxy conflict, which still loomed large on the horizon. A two-year tour had left her starting college at twenty instead of eighteen, and with a limp instead of a spring in her step, but she'd made it, and she felt confident about her chances. Still, she was nervous.

A phone chirped, ringing from seemingly everywhere and nowhere, and when she answered, "Hi, Mom," I heard my own voice projecting through the iRing, and I saw her past unfold. An adoption from a COVID-25–stricken family. The joys and terrors of bringing a young girl into my already-formed family, my husband and I learning how to parent a child who had already lost parents she knew and loved. The teenage fighting that always plays out between mother and daughter had had the undertones of rebellion that only this kind of relationship can give, but also the perfect and yearning love between a chosen parent and a chosen child.

She knew I missed her when she was at school.

"I'll be in the car by four, and at the airport by six. See you by nine."

The ability to get across the country in three hours still amazed me, but it didn't make the distance between Los Angeles and Massachusetts seem any smaller. I imagined her hurtling through the sky, and my old anxieties kicked in, but I told her I couldn't wait to see her, and we hung up.

Tears obscure my vision, and I am back in my mind palace. Thunder reverberates in this space, rain pounding insistently on the window to my right. I peer out, and the blurring of my tears mixes with the blurring of the rain.

## THE WORST OF TIMES

Elizabeth didn't matter.

She remembered mattering, back when her parents were alive. And maybe in the few years after they had died, she'd still mattered some. But now? She didn't matter at all. It started big, but it also started small. When *Roe v. Wade* fell, as we had all known it would, they tried to tell everyone it just meant that states could do what they wanted and that the federal government had no interest in the matter. She remembered, back when girls could go to school, learning about the slave states' making the same argument when the Kansas-Nebraska Act passed and overturned the Missouri Compromise. Even if they didn't teach it anymore, she remembered.

The lie became evident when Massachusetts tried to pass a women's health sanctuary law that prevented extradition of women who left their home states to seek abortions in Boston, one of the few places it was still legal. In *Cruz v. Healey,* the Supreme Court had ruled that Massachusetts had no standing to ignore the criminal law of other states and required the governor to send seven women back to Texas for trial. Each was executed for murder.

Of course there had been outrage, but after the Senate had refused to hold Trump accountable and acquitted him in his second impeachment trial, he had been able to run again in 2024. And win again, because of the armed mobs that shut down critical precincts on Election Day in swing states. Everyone remembered the Seattle mayor's public hanging following her sedition trial, after all. Nobody wanted to be next on the rope. And so people stayed home, kept their heads down, and hoped it would pass.

It was the start of Trump's third term when things started to get worse. COVID-25 wiped out millions, including Elizabeth's parents. Under the leadership of Vice President Miller, access to overwhelmed hospitals was denied to anyone with an incarcerated relative and those who had received public assistance in the past twenty years. When Justice Roberts resigned from the Supreme Court in protest, it just got worse. The "liberal bloc" of the court was then only Elena Kagan and Sonia Sotomayor, and the "originalist justice" Trump nominated floated the idea in his confirmation hearings—still held, if not still meaningful—that nothing in the Constitution permitted women to sit on the bench. Lawsuits were quickly filed, and in just two years, the court agreed. There were no women left in the judiciary.

That's when Massachusetts, California, New York, and a

handful of other states seceded. Right up until the nukes. There were no more secessions after that.

It became so easy for them then. When women—to protect the institution of the American family—were relegated back to their homes, there was no way to say no. Women were prevented from running for office, and those who still served silently stepped aside, letting their husbands take their seats. Since women weren't working, there was no need for women to be educated. Such a bounty for the nation, saving all that money on education that would never be put to use, they said. Women's honored place in the home, their sacred role of domesticity, would be handed down from mother to daughter. In this, there was freedom, they said.

Elizabeth remembered what freedom meant. It did not mean this.

But Elizabeth didn't matter.

*No* was no longer a word in the vocabulary of a woman.

"Yes, I will marry you."

"Yes, I will obey you."

"Yes, I will submit to you."

But that was false, too. *Yes* mattered as much as *no*. A car cannot consent to being driven. What need would a woman have for consent or nonconsent? She was a vessel for the future, carrying a quiver full of patriots and fulfilling the will of her husband. As Elizabeth lay beneath the man her uncle had chosen for her, dreaming of the woman she'd once loved, she did not consent. And it did not matter.

Thunder peals, and I pull back into the two-window room of my mind palace. The tears are no longer blurring my vision; instead they soak my cheeks. I touch my face, and the spell is broken. I am back in my home, the canyon stretching out before me. Warm California air dries my wet face, but my heart will not stop racing. I know these things are not predictions; I know this is not how it will unfold. But each event, each future, each possibility, is based in what *already exists*. As you are reading this, where does *Roe v. Wade* stand? Can you still marry who you want? Did your vote count in the election? Do you matter?

You matter to me. And Ruth Bader Ginsburg mattered to all of us.

Yesterday, I lost a hero. Soon, she will be buried, and a man who did not deserve her and has no business choosing her successor will attempt to do so. To the left, over the Pacific Ocean, just a few miles west of me, bright sun shines across the nation. I feel its warmth. But I see the storm clouds gathering on the right, a dark smear far on the horizon. I feel them roiling, their sick winds filling the sails of uncertain ships. And I miss RBG.

===

# The Sickness in Men

I remember the first time it happened. I made a political statement on Twitter, something reasonably innocuous, like "Maybe it's time to stop killing civilians in the Middle East." I didn't think it was all that controversial, especially in the early days of the Barack Obama presidency, when ending those wars was a national priority that so many of us agreed on. But, it's the internet, and the internet is full of terrible people. This once again played out on full display when a screen grab of me from a movie I had done when I was in my early twenties flashed across the display. I was topless.

"Less talk. More tits." That's it. That was the tweet.

I could have puked. I mean, this was back in the early days of Twitter. The idea of minute-to-minute, real-time interactions between celebrities and fans was pretty new. I'd had a few jerks, but mostly it was the kind of stupidity we still see today. "Your dumb," they would say, not seeing the irony. There was the parade of clichés who spent too much time listening to Rush Limbaugh screeching, "Who's the boss now, Samantha? Your a libtard from hollyweird," and thinking they were original, interesting, and funny. I could reply, "You're," before blocking them and moving on. But this was new. This was using my own body, in one of the most vulnerable moments I had ever experienced on-screen, to shut me up.

And for a minute, it worked.

An icy core burned deep in my stomach, fury and shock, and yes, even shame. Now, I'm not ashamed of my body, and I'm not ashamed of being naked, or being seen naked. But still, this small-minded, hateful little creep nearly sent me running from Twitter, never to return, simply by using my own body—and the idea of me as a woman having any kind of sexuality on display—against me. Never mind that it is exactly because of lowlifes like this man, who almost certainly only go and see movies if the potential for naked women exists in them, that my industry treats women like sexual objects for men to consume. He had taken his own perversions, his own entitlement toward my body, and used it as a political weapon.

I reported the account, and that weak little man was banished from Twitter—a rarity then and now, as Twitter's enforcement of its own harassment policies remains spotty at best. But it wasn't even close to the last. Now it's a daily occurrence, and the more openly political I become, the more actively these idiots try to use my body to silence me. I'm immune to it now, it doesn't hurt, and it sure as hell won't shut me up. But it took years to get there, facing a daily onslaught of sexual violations. And that's what these are—as far as I'm concerned, they are sex crimes, and the men who perpetrate them almost certainly mistreat the women in their own lives.

There is a sickness in men. A sickness of entitlement and power, a corruption that cuts to the soul of who they are. And if you're a man, before you lose your shit and start shrieking, "Not all men, Alyssa," ask yourself these questions: How many times did you look for the hacked iCloud photos of Jennifer Lawrence? Did you watch the Erin Andrews video? When you watch porn—and yes, you watch porn—does it ever involve consent? Have you ever googled your favorite actresses' names followed by "nude"? Have you ever chosen to watch a movie because you thought women were likely to get naked in it? Have you ever pressured an intimate partner to pose for or take nude photos for you? Have you ever shared those photos without her knowledge or consent? Have you ever sent a picture of your penis to a woman without her asking you to?

If you're a man, you almost certainly have done one or more of these things. Your husband, or your son, or your brother, or your father has almost certainly done at least some of these things.

Still not convinced? Just think of our language. There is no equivalent slur to *bitch*. What a demeaning word, rooted in pregnancy and womanhood, reducing women to something less than human. How many times have you called a woman a bitch? Your ex? Your mother-in-law? Maybe your boss? In fact, if you somehow have a woman as a boss, you've almost certainly called her a bitch, or thought it.

There is a sickness in men. If you can't be honest with yourself, you'll never be honest with the women in your life.

I worry about this sickness and what it means for us. I worry that men are so desperate to cling to patriarchy that they will continue to weaponize our sexuality. The real-world consequences of this stretch far beyond assholes on Twitter showing me my breasts and telling me to shut up. I worry that younger women who have been pressured into taking and sending naked photos of themselves will have those photos used against them any time they try to upend the apple cart and get women true equality. I watched my friend Katie Hill lose her congressional seat because *she was the victim* of nonconsensual pornography. Men were so titillated, and so breathlessly *scandalized*, by the actions of an abuser who leaked private photos of her to the media that Katie had to resign. How fucked up is that? And yet, how typical.

"Why did you dress like that? Were you looking for attention?"

"How much did you have to drink?"

"What did you do to lead him on?"

"Less talk. More tits."

There is a sickness in men, and it is sickening our culture.

This male virus, this need to sexualize women's bodies, is so vile that we can't even feed our babies. The mere sight of a female nipple performing its only true function is so risqué that women are forced to hide the act, to cover up their chests and their babies because that same asshole who assaulted me on Twitter might lose his shit if he ever actually encountered a real breast in real life. Just sit back and think for a minute how stupid it is that there has to be a "free the nipple" movement. At least on women, nipples have a purpose. On men, they're just decoration, pinned to a chest nobody wants to look at but they feel free to show around wherever they want. Going swimming? Put your pictures up on Instagram, boys, the nipples are fine. Oh, not you, missy. That's porn.

Come on.

And the thing is, it's men who cause the vast majority of problems in this area. If we went through the phones of most of you men out there, of most of the men in Congress, in the clergy, in the schools, we'd find nude pictures of them. Guarantee it. We all know it. And nobody cares. Scott DesJarlais was elected after news broke that he, an antichoice doctor, had had an affair with a patient, gotten her pregnant, and asked her to get an abortion, then admitted to extramarital sexual affairs with six women, two of whom were his patients. Men are entitled to do these things. Men are insulated from the consequences of doing these things. Men expect women to never do these things.

There is a sickness in men.

Right now, there's an adolescent boy going on Pornhub for the first time. This is how he is going to learn about sex. And because of this male sickness, the most popular videos that will appear on the front page? "Slut Teen Gets Fucked in Hotel Room." "Son Fucks Stepmom's Face." "Hot Teen Babysitter Gets Fucked After Getting Caught Stealing." "Busted!!? Step SISTER Found My Camera After Her Shower." "Stepmom Catches Son Jerking Off with Her Panties." Those are actual titles from Pornhub. This is what you're teaching him, men. This is how he will relate to women. He'll think women are there to fulfill every fantasy he's ever had, and they'll even supply him with the fantasies. He'll never hear a man called a "filthy whore," but he'll hear it an awful lot applied to women. He'll never ask what she likes or if it's okay if he does something.

And he will catch the sickness.

It will get worse as he gets older. It will get worse when he gets on social media and sees men of all political persuasions attacking women for posing for the naked pictures men demand. It's on the right, and it's on the left. It's not political, it's cultural, and it's evil. The men who shame Melania Trump for having naked photos are no different than the men who shame me for being in movies that required nudity. They'll call Katie Hill a slut, and they'll call Ivanka Trump a whore. They'll masturbate in their dank, sweaty basements to the movies I made in my early twenties, and then send me the pictures to try to shame me into silence.

There is a sickness in men.

I go on vacation, I go to the beach, and I have to wonder if there is an asshole with a camera and a telephoto lens somewhere I can't see them. A woman in college has sex with her boyfriend and has to worry if there is an iPhone recording them somewhere in the mess of the dorm room. A woman gets a divorce and has to worry for the rest of her career that her fragile ex-husband will be so broken by the experience that he'll try to end her career with the vestiges of their sex life. And their daughters learn to shut up, to be silent, to be the good girl who lets men do what they want so that they won't try to ruin her life in the future.

"Send me your nudes."

"This whore, sending nude pictures. Look. Look at her tits."

Matt Gaetz, a Congressman from Florida, is said to have passed nudes around Congress of women he claims to have slept with.

They say rape isn't about sex. It's about power. This isn't so different from rape, then. It's degrees, of course, and I don't want to minimize in any way the experience of women who have been raped. But the origins are the same. The genesis, the dark, scared, infected recesses of a man's brain, where he feels entitled to a woman's body—much more than she is— comes from a shared mentality. If a man will use a woman's sexuality to keep a grip on his own power, and so many men will, then there are probably other ways he will do the same. Whether it's overt violence, a shame and harassment campaign like Katie Hill's ex allegedly waged, or the continued exercise of societal power to exclude women from places of power, these men will take the worst path available to them.

James Woods did a nude scene in his early thirties, in a movie called *The Onion Field*. He's also very outspoken on Twitter. Hell, my friend Mark Ruffalo even *offered to do a nude scene if Donald Trump wasn't elected.*

I don't see anyone telling James, "Less talk, more dick." Nobody is telling Mark to "shut up and strip." It doesn't hurt their careers. It wouldn't keep them from running for office or getting another job. But Katie Hill lost her congressional seat, because *she* was a victim. Sarah Silverman was put in a time-out on Instagram because her nipple was visible in a mirror behind the full shelves of a medicine cabinet. But here's what the man elected president revealed just before the election that he won:

"I moved on her like a bitch. But I couldn't get there. And she was married. Then all of a sudden I see her, she's now got the big phony tits and everything . . . you know, I'm automatically attracted to beautiful—I just start kissing them. It's like a magnet. Just kiss. I don't even wait. And when you're a star, they let you do it. You can do anything . . . Grab 'em by the pussy. You can do anything."

There is a sickness in men.

# Mommy,
# That Still Happens?

You've all heard about it: the talk. The talk Black parents must have with their children to try to keep them safe when they interact with police. The talk none of us white people ever need to have. And recently, I had an experience that brought this difference starkly into my life. My five-year-old daughter, Bella, caught me crying. The news of George Floyd's murder—not killing, *murder*—and the heartbreaking video of the act had just played on TV again, from yet another angle. I watched as that man took his last struggling breath, a white knee pressed into his neck. Bystanders pleaded with his murderer to stop. They begged him not to kill George. They warned him of what was happening. And still he pressed, while the three police with him stood around and did nothing to stop it.

These people who are paid to protect us, again, murdered

an unarmed Black man. His alleged crime? Passing a counter-feit $20 bill during a pandemic to buy food. It broke me. I started sobbing in my living room, which is where Bella found me. And so we had the talk about what happened. I told her that a Black man who had done nothing wrong was killed by police. I told her that police should be there for all of us, but that too often they victimize Black people. I told her it was unfair and bad for our country.

After I finished, with tears still pouring down my face and my voice tight and sore from trying to talk through them, she looked at me and said, "Mommy, that still happens?" Part of me wondered at her innocence—it seemed so foreign to her. At five years old, she knew this was wrong; she knew it should never be happening. And so she had relegated it to the past, somewhere in ancient history with my nineties music and World War II and dragons. It didn't make sense, so it couldn't exist in her world.

And this is what my mind keeps coming back to: The question mark after Bella's "Mommy, that still happens?" would be a period or an exclamation point coming from her if we were Black. Our white privilege lives in that punctuation. The idea that we could question whether this happens, that we could tell the tale of police brutality against Black people as a threat to what makes us American as opposed to a threat to what makes us *alive*. That, right there? That's my privilege. You've heard this before, and it probably pissed you off: We're *all* racist. We, white people, *all* benefit from the systemic racism that is inherent in our culture and in our society. If that makes you angry, if your first reaction is to reject that very simple and true statement? That's our white fragility, snowflake. Get over it.

After Trayvon Martin was murdered—and yes, he too was murdered, not killed—and the jury declared his murderer not guilty because of Florida's idiotic "stand your ground" law, President Obama made remarks I thought about again. "Trayvon Martin could have been me thirty-five years ago," he said. "And when you think about why, in the African American community at least, there's a lot of pain around what happened here, I think it's important to recognize that the African American community is looking at this issue through a set of experiences and a history that doesn't go away." Those last few words: *doesn't go away.* It's a thing we white people just can't get our heads around. The generational trauma. The idea that the pain of the grandmother is living in the granddaughter and white people won't do anything mean-ingful to stop the cycle.

Not can't. Won't. How absolutely terrible of us.

None of us, and I mean *none* of us—not me, not you, not a single white person—has done enough. If we had, this would be done. If we had, we wouldn't have a militarized police force in Minneapolis that uses force against Black people seven times more than against white people. We wouldn't have had a president who courts white nationalists in the White House. If police ever had to kneel with protesters, they would not go and pick up their rubber bullets and tear gas five minutes later. There would be no police union executive saying he was "not bothered" by any of the shootings in which he was involved. The exclamation point of Black America following the statement "This still happens" would become the question mark of white America.

We have to do better. All of us.

So what do we do?

First, we have to shut up and listen. Stop telling Black people what they need to do and how to do it. FOLLOW. MUTE. LISTEN. Let our Black leaders lead. Support *their* initiatives. Use your white privilege, which you absolutely do have, only toward its own demise. Look in the mirror and see the microaggressions we all commit, and commit to ending them. Find Black-owned businesses in your community and buy things there. Not just now, when the wounds of George Floyd's murder are all still fresh. But in the months and years to come, when Black people in America think you've forgotten his name.

Too often, we do forget their names.

Stop asking the "safe" Black friend you have how to not be

a racist. Do the work. There are amazing antiracism resource lists all over the internet. Right now, I am rereading *The New Jim Crow: Mass Incarceration in the Age of Colorblindness* by Michelle Alexander. Brittany Packnett Cunningham made me aware of an excellent list of antiracism resources. Go to the Black Lives Matter website and see the work they are doing and have been doing for years. We may be new to this, somehow, but they are not. Now you know where to start, so don't make your Black friend do your work for you. They've done that for four hundred years. That's done. Our work is our work, and we have been absent at this office for a very, very long time. Vacation is *over*. We can and should be angry. We can and should be sad. But don't think for a second that the burden of our anger and sadness is even a tiny bit comparable to the anger and sadness Black people carry, and don't make them lift our anger and sadness too. We need to create white caucuses among our family and friends and have real conversations about race and abolishing racism, or it's just another construct of white supremacy. But those conversations can't be white people asking Black people to do the heavy lifting.

We had a presidential election in 2020, and we'll have midterms in 2022, but frankly, every election matters. And white people? We have homework. We've gerrymandered Black votes out of relevance all across this country. *We* did it. If there's not a Black candidate in one election, we're going to find out why. We're going to find our local community organizations and help *fund* Black candidates. We're going to volunteer for them. We're going to knock on doors in white neighborhoods so they don't have to risk the danger created by our racism, but also, *more* important, because it is part of the work. We need to be missionaries in our own communities, and we need to talk frankly with our own neighbors about the problems we created. If you're thinking about running for a seat on your school board or your city council, how about working to recruit a Black candidate to that seat instead and supporting them from start to finish? We need to give up our power so Black people can live.

The experience of Black people in America won't go away until *we* get over ourselves, *we* put our egos aside, *we* put our money and our hearts and our privilege into this effort. Until we step aside and share our power, not as tokenism, not so we can pat ourselves on the back, but so we can have a truly just and equal society. Until we recommend a person of color for the promotion we ourselves want because it is right, and because the barriers to that person's promotion are too great. Until we step out of all-white boardrooms and classrooms and police forces and bring others who do not look like us in. And not just when thousands of people are screaming at white hearts that aren't listening. But next week. Next month. Next year. Until it *does* go away. And it's not just Black people—Black and brown people across the nation have suffered from hundreds of years of systemic oppression, and *we*, as white people, continue to reap the benefits. While I talk largely about Black people here, the work we have to do expands to all nonwhite people. All.

I hate it. I hate racism. I hate the constant slew of microaggressions we put out in our interactions with Black and brown people. I know that I change the way I talk when I'm with Black women. I start off with "Hey, girl." And I hate that I do it. You do it too, or a collection of things like that. I hate the racist American reality that values my whiteness over anyone else's Blackness. I hate that if I get stopped by the police, my biggest worry is how big the ticket will be, while Black people have to worry about even surviving it. I hate that I'm so much less likely to be stopped, to be searched, to be arrested, to be charged, or to be convicted than Black people.

I hate that the most important words in the Declaration of Independence, "That all men are created equal," are not reflected in our reality. It wasn't reflected for George. For Breonna. For David. For Eric. For Tamir. For Trayvon. For Freddie. For Ahmaud. For Sandra. For Tony. For Malcolm. For Medgar. For Martin. Over and over and over again since the first white boot stomped onto the American coast and the first white ship sailed into an African harbor. I hate it.

But we're not going to win with hate. We'll win with love. I love you. I love this country. I love the patriotism of each of you speaking out to make this country better. And I love fighting alongside you to tear down oppressive systems and build something where all of us are not only created equal but treated equally. And in that love, I'm asking you to take action. To examine yourself, your privilege, your microaggressions, as I will be examining mine. Join actions, like Color of Change's demands for divestment and accountability. Or support the important work that Black Lives Matter is doing. Be missionaries for justice in your neighborhoods. Channel your love into action.

Someday, my Bella may have a daughter of her own. Someday, she may be asked the same question: "Mommy, this still happens?" I want her to be able to say, honestly, "No, kiddo. It used to. It was the worst thing we ever did as a country. But together, we fixed it." I want the question mark to be universal. Stay safe. Stay angry. And stay in touch. I'm here for you, trying to do better every day.

# Cancel Culture
## Is Canceled

Welp, this is going to piss some of you off. Hang in there.

During the 2016 primaries, long before I sent my #MeToo tweet, I endorsed Bernie Sanders for president. I believed then and I believe now that he is a smart man with bold and visionary ideas, and that those ideas should be part of our national discussion. I am to my core a progressive. I believe health care is a human right. I believe that women and minorities should be driving government forward, and that the policies that can best serve all of us are those that help the people who most need them first. I believe in affirmative action, in prison reform, in robust social welfare programs, in actual living minimum wages for everyone. I start from the place of believing women when they make claims of sexual assault against powerful men. I think college should be free, student loan debt forgiven, and an education, whether academic or trade, of equal quality made equally accessible to everyone.

And in 2016, I saw a perfect opportunity to enact these goals at the presidential level. Like many of us, I could not believe that Donald Trump—or any of a very weak, regressive, and intellectually challenged Republican field of candidates—could win the Oval Office. Their primary process was almost a comedy. A hateful, poorly written comedy, but a comedy nonetheless. It was absurd. Here we had a person becoming the front-runner in a national election talking about the size of his penis during a debate and *winning*. In my view, the general was going to be a cakewalk for whoever the nominee would be, and so I threw my heart and soul into the Bernie campaign.

And we lost. I quickly came to support Hillary Clinton, because while she wasn't my first choice, she was smart, bold, more qualified than any candidate in my lifetime, and excited and inspired so many people. That's how primaries work—we come together as a party to make a collective decision. Some people don't get their first choice, but we had a truly good and competent second choice. I was proud to support her.

And holy shit, did it get ugly.

I know many of you will say that Bernie Bros are a myth. I call bullshit. Never while supporting Bernie did I receive the hate and derision and vitriol from Hillary supporters that I received from Berners immediately upon announcing my support for her. People started attacking me personally, saying I was the exact opposite of everything I am. They said I wanted to take away their health care. They said I wanted to make sure the big banks ran everything and that I hate poor people. Get this: They (almost exclusively men) called me a bad feminist for *endorsing a woman*. And people tried to get #AlyssaMilanoIsCanceled trending.

Here's the thing: Cancel culture is a joke. It's an expression of entitlement and arrogance, the complete rejection of the simple notion that people who share your values can approach them in a different way than you do. And that's at its best. At its worst, and largely at its core, it is the idea that people who have a microphone are not entitled to make mistakes or have opinions that vary from yours even slightly. It's preposterous. It's childish, divisive, conceited, and Trumpian to its core.

When I say something, I think about what I say before I say it. But I'm human, and like everyone else, I know I don't always get it right. I remember one tweet I sent on International Women's Day. I made the mistake of going into my Twitter mentions, and a Trump troll named Kirk asked if I was transgender. He was trying to insult me, not smart enough or evolved enough to realize there was nothing insulting about calling someone trans. Now, I knew there was nothing I could say that would change this person's heart, but

I hoped I could speak up in solidarity to help other people be seen. And so I replied to him with the following:

*I'm trans. I'm a person of color. I'm an immigrant. I'm a lesbian. I'm a gay man. I'm the disabled.*

*I'm everything. And so are you, Kirk.*

*Don't be afraid of what you don't know or understand.*

*No one wants to hurt you. We are all just looking for our happily ever after.*

This came from a place of solidarity. My intent was to say that we are all human, we all share the same spirit and heart and have hopes and dreams, and the small biological factors that weak-minded people use to divide us are immaterial. But, as people I respect and who know and respect me told me both privately and publicly, this made them feel like I was stealing their lived experience. And I listened to them, and I heard them, and I explained myself and apologized to anyone I hurt with these words. This is how we grow and do better. This is the way to do things.

But the frothy-mouthed vitriol I took from people on the far left was indistinguishable from what I got from the right. Alt-left Twitter and alt-right Twitter joyfully danced together in my mentions, Twitchy and Gab and Parler loyalists high-fiving their counterparts on our side of the ideological divide.

"Alyssa is canceled" was their message. From the same people who say "Eat the rich" without a trace of irony.

Now, I'm tough. I can take it. Mostly, I sit back and laugh at the absurdity of all of it. But I worry that people who want to get involved, who want to speak out and push our dialogue forward, won't do so because they see just how *mean* the cancel culture keyboard warriors are. I can imagine a young woman who has something to say, who desperately wants to speak her mind and share in solidarity with a progressive landscape, keeping her mouth shut, staying silent, because of the treatment I and other visible women receive from these hateful people. And it is mostly women who receive this treatment, whom those on the far left and the far right try to silence. They rarely have anything to say about Harvey Weinstein, though, unless they are trying to tie him to political figures they want to silence.

Burning deep in the heart of this subculture is patriarchy. It is fueled by a sad desire to silence women who don't precisely conform to someone's entrenched vision of what feminism or progressivism or just basic political speech in America should be. We're told by a male-dominated political system to toe their line or shut up, and we're also shouted at by some of the people who say they want to overturn this system to shut up and toe *their* line instead. It's all the same; silencing women is what patriarchy is all about.

You know, people have been trying to cancel me in one form or another since the late 1980s. I'm still here, working in Hollywood and the public eye. Many of them are not. I won't sit back and let that young woman who sees these vultures be intimidated into silence. I won't accept that people can't make mistakes and grow, and I especially don't accept the notion that disagreeing about the techniques we use to achieve the *same desired goals* gives anyone the right to shame someone into silence.

My daughter, Bella, will someday google me. It's the nature of the beast, but I so dread that day. I've worked for thirty years to make the world a better place, starting as a teenager. In that time, I've grown. I've evolved. I've fucked up, and I've always tried to learn from it. I'll fuck up again, and I'll try to grow from that. The growth is the only difference between me and the people trying to silence me—they forgive their own mistakes but nobody else's. And a lot of what Bella sees when she does look for me on the internet will be these sad bullies trying to paint her mother as a bad person who should shut up and look pretty on the screen.

Well, fuck that, and fuck you if you think I'm going to. Or that *any* person who disagrees with you should shut up and go away. The difference between calling people out and calling people in—people of good intentions who are working to do the right work the right way but sometimes make mistakes—is one of arrogance. Now, I'm not talking about people with hateful views who use their platforms to promote those views—the Nazis, the Proud Boys, the Trumps. Instead, I'm talking about people who have demonstrated their intentions, who have the potential to learn and the desire to listen. The people trying to "cancel" right-intentioned allies who choose the wrong word or through ignorance say the wrong thing are generally at least as problematic as the person they are trying to cancel.

Because to them the messenger is more important than the message. If they've decided the messenger isn't their ideal, rather than accept their good intentions, they tear that person down. They don't care that it sets their goals back, and they care even less that it actively hurts people. They can thrive in the self-satisfied smugness of *rightness* as the world burns around them. It's pathetic.

It got worse when I endorsed Joe Biden in 2020. I remained neutral for nearly the entire Democratic primary process. I believed then and believe now that we had a field of smart, qualified candidates with big ideas, and every one of them would be light-years better than Donald Trump to lead our nation. I raised money for everyone from Marianne Williamson to Pete Buttigieg. I was not going to tear down anyone, because I wanted to be able to support the eventual nominee with my full heart and my loudest voice. But finally, it became apparent that Joe was going to win the nomination, and Bernie still wouldn't drop out. And I called him out on it. I said it was time to unify behind the nominee who could beat Trump.

You know, Bernie called me early in his 2020 campaign and asked me to endorse him. I told him the issues I had with his 2016 campaign, including the vitriol of some of his most ardent followers. I called out the divisiveness, and the consequences of that divisiveness. I told him his failures to manage these problems were so damaging, in the hope that he would rise above them in 2020. I did this privately; I never made public complaints about him. I called him in, instead of calling him out.

And I never heard back.

I've said it all along: Beating Donald Trump was the most important goal in 2020. His election was an existential threat to America. Because of his Supreme Court appointments, I believe millions of women will lose the right to make their own reproductive health care decisions. The gerrymandering that started under the George W. Bush administration will become so protected, so dug in, that we will basically have single-party rule in America for generations. Every basic human right is at risk, and I can't take it. I can't let it happen. And so, when it became apparent that Joe Biden was going to be the nominee, I started saying loudly that it was time for the party, and all candidates in the race, to get behind him. And the alt-left lost their minds. I was called a "corporate whore." I was told to shut up over and over again. Allegedly progressive people, mostly men, sent vile, misogynistic, and threatening messages to me, because I wanted the most progressive possible outcome for the election. It was chilling. This is what privilege and entitlement look like. This is what patriarchy looks like. And it is exactly what cancel culture looks like.

None of this is to say anyone gets a free pass. Intent matters. There's no room for racism or lies or rape enabling. None. There's no room for Harvey Weinstein—but guess what? That sonofabitch was canceled by a jury of his peers. We canceled the racist in the White House at the ballot box. Their intent is and has always been to harm. But when people of good intentions use a poor turn of phrase or speak from a place of wanting to help but not fully understanding an issue, for fuck's sake, we can help them understand. We can support and educate them. We can appreciate their intent and guide them to the best expression of that, with kindness and empathy and common cause.

Activism is about bringing about change. Ultimately, that will come through unity. Sure, we'll need to steamroll some people who are unwilling to listen, who are desperate to cling to outdated, wrong, and hateful ideologies. But through uniting people of good heart and good intention, through education and connection, this is how we have always made change. James Reeb, a white minister and activist, joined the Black

Freedom Riders and was killed in Birmingham in 1965. He was called in. George W. Bush and Michelle Obama are legitimately friends, after all. We can find unity, find common cause, and find progress even across great divides. We can forgive trespasses—especially those that come from a place of love and a place of progress. And together, we can shape the world, but it gets so much harder if we don't cancel cancel culture.

# Bella

My sweet Bella,

Years from now, when you think back to this time in your life, I want you to remember the pandemic we lived through. The good and the bad—and no matter what you hear, no matter what you're taught about it, and no matter what happens between now and when you're old enough to read this, there was plenty of both during this strange and scary time.

We were so lucky. I mean it. So, so lucky. But a lot of other people weren't. Hundreds of thousands of people died agonizing deaths, many of them alone, many of them terrified. People drowned in their own mucus while half of the country tried to pretend the pandemic wasn't even real. Whole cities were shut down, and people fought over toilet paper. Small businesses closed, never to reopen again. Some big businesses too. This put such a strain on our economy and our standing in the world. What's really sad about it is that the very richest people got even richer while the rest of the world got so much poorer. We saw everything that is broken in capitalism under the brightest, most revealing light, and as usual the people who had the least suffered the most. I want you to remember that millions of people, including people we love, had to work in unsafe environments, risking their health as essential workers just to keep food on the table.

But there you and Milo were. As you took your afternoon naps less and less frequently, I would lean my head on your doorjamb, watching your chest rise and fall in gentle breaths, and wonder if there was any way I was doing this parenting thing right at all. I've always been a worrier, even in the best of times. Raising children during a pandemic wasn't something I had prepared for, or had ever really considered. I'd traveled the world and seen such suffering in so many families, but never had I imagined the problems that hurt so many people around the world would exist here in the United States as well. I hope that as you're reading this, it is a distant memory tucked away somewhere between that time Milo had to get his eye glued shut because of the golf ball incident and the time you stepped on a bee and your little toe swelled up.

It's important to know everything I'm telling you. It's important to internalize it, to make better choices than your mom's generation did when we had the chance to decide. But the things I want you to *remember* are different. They are the things that I hope you can look back on in the dark of your own personal fears and know that you have connections deeper and more powerful than anything the world can throw at you. I want you to remember the countless nights you slept in my bed as the world outside ground to a halt. We stayed up late watching movies or your weird slime videos (just ew). On those nights, Daddy slept in the guest room. He understood we needed to hold each other—he wasn't getting away, he was giving us a place to be connected in the special way you and I connect. I want you to remember our dogs. You loved them so. They were so happy we were home with them all day. And I want you to remember the day we brought Halo home—his bright blue eyes burning with play and curiosity and love for his new family. I want you to remember me and Dad working from home and meeting in the kitchen for lunch and a smooch. And the slow dances with you in between us.

On Saturdays, our favorite day of the week, remember that we picked flowers from our garden and made homemade turmeric tea to keep everyone healthy. Remember that Dita and Papa, Uncle Alaa and Uncle Coco, Charlie and Luke would come over to play in the backyard. It was the only time we saw each other during quarantine because of the virus. And we couldn't kiss or get close to each other (although Dita always broke the rules just to smell you, hug Milo, and kiss Luke's toes). Every week, Daddy picked up sandwiches and we would all be together for a few hours. Little Luke thought our house was Disneyland, which I guess made you a princess and me Minnie Mouse. I'll never understand why it was called social distancing. It should have been called physical distancing and social connecting. I want you to remember the rock and roll party we had over Zoom where your aunt Sissy got dressed up like a rock star and made a guitar out of a broom.

You didn't know it then, but you were closer to your family then than most families ever get to be, even at a time when we were farthest apart in so many ways. You had the gift of time with people who love you more than you can imagine. That was time I never got with my parents and grandparents when I was little, and it is time I relished reclaiming with you, watching generations of our family come together and learn, truly learn, how little we could take for granted, and how precious we are to one another.

Every night at five thirty we would do a family FaceTime just so we could watch your baby cousin Luke eat his dinner. "Bella! Bella!" he would yell when he saw you, and you laughed so hard every time. We had movie nights outside with your friends, wearing masks and keeping enough distance that we would feel safe enough to let our guard down just a little bit. I wonder how this will affect you when you're grown. As a grown-up Bella, do you wipe down the groceries? Do you use so much hand sanitizer that your hands are constantly dry? I swear my hands have aged a million years since this thing started. Speaking of aging, I didn't dye my hair once the pandemic started. But I did take up new worries, like wiping down all the groceries, keeping us in a bubble in our home, and the new wrinkles that took up residence in the corners of my eyes. You used to cuddle on my lap and try to smooth them as we got ready for bed. I'm sorry if all this made you neurotic. Your dad and I did the best we could. We were so scared.

I also want you to remember our family road trip. The four of us in a stinky, tiny RV with about fifteen of your baby dolls. You even brought your sequined pillow from your room so the RV looked pretty. The hours on the road in that rickety RV were some of the happiest times of my life. You and your brother curled up together to nap while your dad and I listened to Crosby, Stills and Nash on the radio singing about teaching your children well and tried not to wake you up while we sang along.

And when you were awake, you would scoot all the way to the back and play music on your iPod and look out the window in wonder at the passing scenery. You were so young, and at five years old everything looked new—because to you, it was. "Mom," you'd exclaim, "look at that volcano! Mama, look at that cactus." The nights were just as special as the days.

We camped out in the cool spring air by fires that your dad made after teaching you and Milo how to gather the right kindling and put the logs in the perfect arrangement. Far away from the lights of the city, the stars hung so bright and big they looked like you could unscrew them and put them in your pocket. You really wanted to make s'mores, but in true Mama fashion I'd only brought mini marshmallows (no chocolate, no graham crackers, and no skewers). You let me off the hook and ate mini powdered doughnuts by the fire instead as we told stories and sang songs and looked up into the mysteries of heaven. Socially distanced from the rest of the world, closer together than ever.

Your brother had a harder time during the pandemic. He had spent years in school already before you got there and knew more clearly the many things he was missing. There is some truth to the old cliché that ignorance is bliss, and so while you were able to play around the house and mostly live the life you had before, Milo could not. He missed his friends and his classes and had a hard time adjusting to the changing expectations that the pandemic placed on us. You were so patient with him even though he drove you mad sometimes. His days were spent playing *Fortnite* as he FaceTimed with his friends, trying to make the best of a truly hard time. And yeah, I let him play longer than I would have otherwise. But shooting weird digital creatures with weird digital weapons made him happy. This was not easy for me, let me tell you. All of this happened during a time in our history (I'm hoping this issue is fixed now) when our country also had a terrible gun violence problem. So many of my friends had children or parents or loved ones who had been shot by real guns in the real world, so the thought of my son's loving this game of course drove me nuts. But I let him do it because all I wanted was for you both to find happiness in a year that was taking so much of it from so many. I wanted each of you to have memories of this time that were more than the losses. I was just trying to keep you both happy.

In the end, my brilliant, creative girl, I want you to remember this the most: When things were the worst in the world that they had been in my lifetime, the planet forced us to slow down so that we could hear the birds singing. Its methods were crude, and painful, and ignored by many of the people who could have done something to make it better. But I want you to remember the songs those birds sang. I want you, and the people you take with you as your chosen family, to share them, to carry their beauty, to make sure you are always listening. Protecting them, honoring them, revering the beauty in the air, will inform the way you treat all of us, the way you elect leaders, the way you reshape our culture.

Your memories will carry this time into the future. They

will be the stories your children, should you have them, will tell their children. In your memory lies the key to happiness and survival and connection when the world slows down again. So think, Bella. Wish. Breathe. Remember.

I love you.

≡

# Around the World
# and Back Again

One of the unexpected responsibilities and opportunities my life has afforded me was the ability to serve around the world as a UNICEF ambassador and with the USO. It's made me realize both how lucky we are in the United States and how much we are one people around the world. I've come to understand that borders do far more to divide us than unite us, not only keeping people out but keeping wealth in. As I write this, I've just read that American billionaires gained more than $1 trillion in net worth during the pandemic, and it brought to mind so much of the suffering I've seen at home and abroad in my career.

I once took an AIDS test at the UNICEF health center in Angola, Africa. I was there on a field visit as a UNICEF goodwill ambassador. "Field visit" is really just a nice way of saying "witnessing hardships like you've never seen before and will never be able to unsee." It was 2004, and this particular trip was my first, just two years after a peace treaty ended the bloody civil war in Angola. There was no infrastructure. There was no government to speak of. There was just suffering.

The people at UNICEF tried to prepare me. It was ten times worse than I could possibly have imagined.

There's something amazing about people in developing nations. It's universal, not unique to Angola, that the people always seem to be right on the edge of laughing or crying. It's a very fine line. There's a fluid fragility that is palpable. They can break at any moment, and sometimes the moment of being seen by someone from America can cause one of these big emotional breaks. For anyone with even the slightest bit of empathy, these moments, these brief connections with total strangers, become the new road map for your own personal well-being.

Angola was in a unique position because of its isolation. In fact, during its long war there was only one road in or out of the country. The result of this was that the AIDS epidemic hadn't spread there like it had on the rest of the continent. But it also meant that people didn't know about it. What government there was and UNICEF were collaborating to educate people as quickly as humanly possible in an all-out effort to spare these long-suffering people the ravages of AIDS that other African nations were experiencing.

I learned all this from a man named James as we bounced along a broken road in an open and sputtering old Jeep. It was on this same ride that I also learned that the red wooden stakes on the side of the road meant there was an active minefield on the other side.

"No weapon should outlast a war," James told me. Imagine driving to work next to an active minefield that your government does nothing about. That's what James's life was like. He continued to educate me about life in Angola—how people struggled to find food and safety and health care. How there was almost no education for the children, and how even the most basic things, like shelter, were hard to come by for many people. There was no work, and there was never enough food.

But nothing James said could have prepared me for the moment when a woman whom I'll call Lerato (to protect her privacy) walked into the clinic. She had a fragile, breakable, but beautiful smile on her face. Another one that could have had tears or laughter hiding just behind it. She couldn't have been any older than fifteen but her eyes were at least thirty. She looked at us with those older eyes and began to speak Portuguese to the women who worked at the clinic. Her voice was soft, the whisper of pencil across dry paper. I could tell by the tsking sound one of the nurses was making that her situation was serious.

As the nurse ambled to a nearby supply room, I followed with James in tow to interpret.

"Is she okay?" I asked.

A flurry of Portuguese followed, James and the nurse talking back and forth in staccato bursts of words that felt like they lasted forever. Finally James looked at me and said, "She is here for an AIDS test. She was raped."

My whole body began to shake. I'm not just saying that because it's something to write that sounds like a real reaction. No. My entire body started shaking. I had to do something. So I went into where Lerato was waiting and I told James to translate this sentence: "Don't be scared. I will take the test with you. We will do it together." And we did. This experience changed me at a fundamental level.

Also in Angola, I marveled at women with their babies tied to them, carrying huge jugs, many of them barefoot, like it was nothing. I bitch if I leave my yoga mat in the car and have to run back out to get it because of the three flights of stairs at the gym. What a lesson in privilege. The whole time I was thinking, "How do these poor people go without water here? How do they walk five miles to get lifesaving water to use to cook and bathe for their families every day?" At the time, it seemed like a complete failure of society—how could any government, no matter how dysfunctional, not make sure its people at least had clean water?

And then the Flint water crisis happened. A whole city, abandoned by an industry. A whole people, poisoned by the most basic of needs, abandoned by their government. I sat and I watched it unfold, and I cried. It made no sense—we're so rich. We tell ourselves we're the best, the most advanced, the freest nation in the world, but we can't even give people clean, safe water to drink. Pipes around the country are more than one hundred years old. From Newark to New Mexico, this basic necessity is not accessible, as aging pipes and out-dated systems leach lead and other contaminants into the water. For poor people, at least. Brown people especially. It disgusts me.

Another lesson in privilege.

The women I saw in Angola and who walked five miles to get clean water would later be my inspiration to raise money for Charity: Water, a nonprofit that was building clean water wells in Ethiopia. Eventually, with a lot of begging on my social media, we raised enough money to build eighteen of those lifesaving wells.

It turns out many of the things I've seen abroad are not at all unlike the problems we have here in America. And that breaks my heart. And pisses me off. Because we could be everything we aspire to be. We have the resources and the talent and the goodness about us. We just lack the will.

I visited India shortly after the 2005 tsunami. In India, I

vaccinated children with the same vaccinations the suburban, yoga-loving antivaxxers in this country have deemed unsafe. Women would wait in line for hours to get their children vaccinated, to keep them healthy. I also saw families who had lost everything celebrating and dancing as they rebuilt their communities even stronger than before, with safer, more modern construction and infrastructure. It's amazing to me, humanity's ability to hope and dream and pick ourselves up and start anew.

I think about this when I look at some of our communities here in the United States. Towns that have been devastated by fires and hurricanes. People who have had to leave everything they knew and loved. In 2018, the California fires burned right up to my property line. The underbrush on one side of my fence was scorched black, but luckily nothing on my side. I know just how lucky I am. I know I have the resources to leave, and while I would be crushed, I would also be okay if the worst happened and I did lose my home. But I also know that most are not so lucky.

In Africa, I heard the wails of a mother as her tiny child—a skeleton with skin—lay across her lap, unable to move as he died of starvation. An image that will still invoke a panic attack if I linger on the memory too long. I think of her pain. The pain of not being able to feed your child because you too are starving yourself and your milk has dried up.

But right here in Iowa—America's cornfield—one in seven kids lives in hunger. As our governments cut access to free and reduced-cost meals in schools, this remarkable and easily addressed injustice will only get worse. What happens in Africa happens here, although we have a better capacity to manage some of the effects of those problems because of our national wealth. But hope for a brighter tomorrow happens everywhere.

I have been to many places and seen the commonality of the struggles of humanity. The thing I haven't seen much of in the rest of the world is people dying from lack of access to for-profit health care. I've sure seen that here. I've been honored to know desperately ill and disabled people who fight with literally their last breaths to ensure everyone has access to health care—even after they themselves are gone. Like my friend Ady Barkan.

Ady is dying from ALS. It's such a cruel disease. It leaves his mind, his beautiful, powerful mind, fully intact. But it is slowly paralyzing his body. It's robbing him of his ability to move, to speak, to breathe. To hold his newborn baby daughter and play with his young son. And in the middle of this, right as he was learning how to die while still being a husband and father and one of the best and most effective activists I've ever met, his insurer denied claims for medical equipment he needed to breathe. Despite the approval of Ady's doctors and the clear and frequent use of these machines for ALS patients in the United States and around the globe, his insurance company called ventilators for ALS patients "experimental." It's a tactic for-profit insurers use throughout the country to deny paying for needed care, buffering their bottom lines with human suffering.

They knew they only had to wait Ady out.

Now, Ady fought back. He sued, and he launched a massive public pressure campaign that ultimately forced his insurer to relent. But he never should have had to do this. He should have been free to spend whatever last days he has left with his family and loved ones, and doing the things he loves.

In so many places around the world, places that are so much poorer than we are, Ady would have received that ventilator, along with all medications and nursing coverage required, for free. And it's not just ALS. Diabetes, cancer, heart disease, and many other chronic illnesses are treated by societies that by all Western standards are considered poor or developing.

What it comes down to, what matters about all of this, is that these are all human stories, and suffering happens everywhere. As Americans, we hold ourselves up as examples to the world. We call our president the "leader of the free world." But the issues we face are universal. They always affect the most vulnerable populations more than anyone else.

Eric Trump has clean water no matter where he travels. Jeff Bezos has access to health care anywhere in the world. And so should you. Human suffering should not be reserved for the poor, nor human rights for the rich.

"People over profits" has to be the driving philosophy of the twenty-first century.

For Ady. For the people I met in India. For the people of Flint.

For Lerato.

My test was negative. Lerato's test was positive. We have to do better.

# To My Fan-ily

I know. Right now you're more than halfway through reading this book and are a little sad it's not full of behind-the-scenes info about *Charmed,* or tidbits of information about my relationships with the actors I've worked with, or really about my work as an actor at all. And that's okay. Because you're still here, reading this book. And that is what I love about my fans, about you: You stick with me, no matter where I go. You've supported my work as an artist *and* as an activist. It gives me space and freedom to be the person I am meant to be, and I'm so grateful to you for that.

When you've been in the business as long as I have, it's easy for the person behind the characters to disappear. Take a peek at my mentions on any social media platform—people call me "Pheebs," or "Samantha," or, more recently, "Coralee." Sometimes people do this to diminish me intentionally. These are usually the trolls who have nothing better to do than try to silence women. But there are others who claim to be fans of me but don't give me my own agency. They don't see Alyssa; they see the characters Alyssa played. I get it, I really do. I know that people love shows and characters and feel a connection to them, and I've been truly honored to be a part of bringing that connection to so many people for so long. But it doesn't leave a lot of space for me to exist. When people call me "Phoebe," they erase so many of the things that make me who I am. Phoebe didn't marry my husband. She didn't have my two sweet, smart, life-affirming children. And she didn't have you—the fans who have made it possible for me to bring you all of those characters. It makes me sad, sometimes.

But what never makes me sad, what never pushes me away, is the vast majority of you who are there for *me*. I appreciate how so many of you take the time out of your lives not just to watch my acting, but to pay attention to my activism. You dive into my podcast no matter what we're talking about, and listen and learn alongside me. So many times, you've given your time, and your money, and your whole hearts to causes I've shared with you, and sometimes you've shared important causes with me.

You are the reason I'm able to do all of the things that I do, and I'm so grateful.

So while I'm not sorry there's not a lot of the behind-the-scenes of your favorite shows in this book, I do see you, and I love you so much for sticking here beside me anyway. Honestly, I just don't feel comfortable tossing out dirty (or even freshly washed) laundry from TV shows that affects other people. The thing about all of us is that we change. We have the capacity to learn and to get better. A lot of people take those opportunities. A few don't. But for me to dredge up those stories about who people used to be may just not be fair to them now. I don't really want to do it. And I don't think, in the end, you really want me to, either. Part of what makes TV and movies magic is that we can see past the actors to the characters on the screen. I worry a bit that digging too deeply into what happened off-camera may diminish so much of what you love on the screen.

I don't want to lift the curtain and in the process hurt your love of the shows we worked so hard to create. I love that love. It's special. Just like you.

What I want to say more than anything to you—yes, specifically you, holding this book—is thank you. Thank you for all you do for me. For fighting the trolls in my comments. For watching the shows. For reading my books and showing up at my book signings, some of you even coming from overseas. For sharing your successes with me, and your challenges. For always showing up when I need you. For giving me the gift of freedom to be the person I want to be. And for working with me to make life better. You are a piece of magic in my world.

# The Everyday Constitution

Nobody alive in 1997 had experienced a presidential impeachment. Now, in just the Trump administration alone, we've experienced two. It's a sad and painful moment for our country, but the exercise is such an important part of the Constitution, and it breaks my heart that the partisan Republican hacks in the Senate ignored their constitutional mandate and left Donald Trump in office after the first impeachment and refused to convict him for inciting the Capitol riot.

Historic tales of what the Framers intended and the meaning of democracy are important, but they can make the Constitution seem like a dusty document with old-fashioned language that is distant from our everyday lives. And it can be hard to express passion and sympathy for an old document. Maybe this is why we turned up in huge numbers to protest for health care and in support of Christine Blasey Ford when she shared her brave testimony about her sexual assault at the hands of a nominee to the Supreme Court, but not so much for the impeachment hearings and trial of a dangerously corrupt president.

People may not guess this, but I have a deep and abiding love for constitutional law—to the point where I've been studying it with a con law professor in my spare time. Many nights after the kids are tucked in, safely asleep, and Dave is immersed in a baseball game on TV, I'll pull out the Constitution, or a volume of the writings of John Jay. I love the vision the Framers expressed in this malleable, forward-looking document. For sure, it reflected their own imperfections and the deep failings of our culture at the time. It ensconced slavery, ignored women, and created an electoral college that ensures white rural voters hold dramatically more power than urban voters of color, even to this day. But it also did something remarkable: It acknowledged its own shortcomings, that the future would look different than the world in which it was written, and gave us the power to change it. We have changed it, twenty-seven times so far. The entire text, from the original writings to the amendments that made it better, matters in our lives today. And it is in this context, through both the long lens of history and the close-up of today, that I want to look at this document and why it's worth fighting for, even now, when forces in our own government seem hell-bent on ignoring it to protect an incompetent executive.

I think we all know about the Bill of Rights—those first ten amendments that clarify or enshrine many of our individual freedoms. We understand that because of those rights, I can say, "Donald Trump, the twice-impeached president of the United States, is an incompetent grifter and Russian stooge and I can't wait to see him and the treasonous, anti-American senators who were too cowardly to do their duty to remove him from office all lose their next elections at the hands of voters who are much, much more patriotic than they are." And I can say it on my way to temple, or church, or an atheist party, in Planned Parenthood or in an op-ed. After that, it gets a bit murky for a lot of us—despite some people's insisting they know exactly what the founders intended.

I mean, who thinks about whether the government would quarter soldiers in their home, like the Third Amendment protects us against? Well, let's say you live anywhere on the southern border, and a racist, authoritarian president saw political gain in using the military illegally against migrants crossing that border. Do you honestly think that terrible president would not have your home full of heavily armed soldiers—housed at your expense—if he was not specifically barred from doing so in the Constitution?

How about if you refused those soldiers? Do you not think

that that same president—a man who called for the execution of five innocent Black teenagers in a full-page ad in *The New York Times*—would shy away from cruel and unusual punishment intended to make sure other homeowners did not also refuse? He certainly didn't do the same when (white) Bernhard Goetz shot four teens on the New York City subway in 1984, nor when (also white) "Son of Sam" went on his killing spree. The man who fetishizes the separation of families, the jailing of immigrant children? Well, the Third Amendment promises that no president can force you to quarter soldiers in your home.

And now, in the shadow of the coronavirus, the Tenth Amendment takes on an even more critical role, relegating the powers not specifically assigned to the federal government to the states. When an incompetent, deadly, and dangerous president says that he is the person with the sole power to reopen a national economy despite the overwhelming scientific advice and evidence saying that this would be a bad idea, we have a document that clearly says he is wrong.

The right likes to think it's co-opted patriotism. They'd like you to believe that the more flags they have flying off the backs of their pickups, the more patriotic they are. No matter how big the flag, it's not a measure of patriotism. Patriotism is about finding our shared national values in the words of the Constitution. It's about living those values, and when we find a failing in that beautiful, imperfect document, fighting to change it. We show up. We get loud—not threatening. Not with guns. With our voices and votes and presence. Every damn time.

It was because of my patriotism, and the power the Constitution vests in that patriotism, that I sat in Congress several times in the past few years, exercising my right as an American to observe my government in action. Each time it felt like I was watching a war between those who love the Constitution and those who want to disregard or manipulate it. I watched the confirmation hearing of Brett Kavanaugh and the acrimony that surrounded it, including a Republican Judiciary Committee caucus that refused to directly question Dr. Blasey Ford themselves because she was a woman and they were all men. I saw a Republican House refuse to hold a hearing on the Equal Rights Amendment even though at the time it had almost reached the threshold for ratification (it has since crossed that threshold), because Congress established an unnecessary and arbitrary deadline for passing the ERA. And I watched an impeachment hearing where Adam Schiff and other impeachment managers made impassioned arguments on behalf of the Constitution as a president and his representatives acted to shred it. It was simultaneously depressing and inspiring, and it made clearer than ever the importance of our founding document. I know who was more patriotic on those committees. Hint: It wasn't the Republicans.

The Constitution is our armor against the slings and arrows of a petty wannabe tyrant and his cronies. And it works to make sure each of us continues to have access to that armor as our population changes and grows and evolves. And it is this very power, this constitutionally mandated tally and response to the changing demographics of our culture, that terrifies the white nationalists in the Trump regime and their backers so much. We get to count the people of color in our nation, and once we count them, we vest them with power.

Article I, section II, of the Constitution reads, "[An] enumeration shall be made . . . within every subsequent Term of ten Years." It might not sound like much, but this is the heart of the power of the American voter: the census. It determines the number of elected federal representatives each state has, along with the number of electors who choose the president for each state. If you don't think these matter, ask Should-Have-Been-President Hillary Clinton, who received more than three million more individual votes than Donald Trump. The Constitution places the power directly in the hands of the people to elect their representatives in Congress, yet Republicans from the very, very gerrymandered

congressional districts around the nation are constantly trying to take this power away from us and put it in the hands of
their political party.

Ultimately, the Constitution is a guide to keep building
America as we grow and change and evolve. It provides us
with a path we can take to help the country evolve, even
though we have to do the work ourselves. It limits the power
of government and hands all power not specifically given to
the government to the people. It's right there in the Ninth and
Tenth Amendments. But people like Donald Trump, people
who have no regard for the document and want to build an
America that rewards people like him while leaving the rest of
us to fend for ourselves, simply ignore it and try to corrupt the
system for their own gain. We need to ask ourselves if we are
okay with that.

I am not. Neither should you be.

The Constitution matters. It matters in terms of how you
live, where you live, how you work, the sovereignty of your
property, and even the sovereignty of your mind and your
body. It (since the Thirteenth Amendment, at least) says that
all Americans are their own owners and can live freely in the
manner they choose so long as that aligns with the narrow
power the government is granted to regulate people's personal lives. But if we don't stand up and fight for this sovereignty, if we in our apathy allow power-hungry politicians

like those in the Trump regime to take those basic rights from us for their own political gain, then it's just another piece of paper—no more and no less.

The Constitution is a living document. And as such, it must be cared for, tended to, and fed with our patriotism. It is not immortal. If we don't protect the Constitution, it will die and take democracy with it.

I love this country. I love this idea of a nation with roots stretching back thousands of years to the earliest democratic governments, stretching all the way back to the Magna Carta and the Code of Hammurabi. But what I really love is how it lives outside of that context and in the world we inhabit today. We simply cannot let this concept die because we were too corrupt, too lazy, too uninformed, and too tired to defend against all the assaults on it.

This is how we secure, as the preamble of the Constitution puts it, the blessings of liberty to ourselves and our posterity.

# A Conversation

I have this recurring daydream. It comes on me at the strangest moments, often in times of conflict or uncertainty. It fills
me when I've lost my faith in people, when I think we can't
possibly find spaces in which we can come together and the
divisions in our world seem so great that there is no bridge
wide enough to span them. And I know it's not real, it's not
something that's happened, but it feels like something that
*could* happen. It restores me a little, and leaves me feeling
hopeful that there are better possibilities out there than what
we're experiencing right now.

It goes like this: I've just finished my annual screen at my
local Planned Parenthood, and I pass through the crowds of
hateful people screaming at me and the other women leaving
the building that we're going to hell and that our babies are
already there. It sickens me, viscerally. I see one man, white

and bearded, small flecks of spittle flying from his mouth as he screams that I'm a baby killer. But behind him, over his shoulder, is an older woman. She's maybe seventy, with white curls packed tightly against her head, which is bowed reverently. I see her flinch as the man shouts. She's dressed too warmly for the weather, and small beads of sweat gather on her face before rolling down its thick lines. I focus on her as I escape from the gauntlet, not making eye contact with the vicious man.

A few blocks away is a coffee shop. I want to shake off the energy of the experience before I go home to my kids, so I grab an iced tea and sit at the bar in the window of the crowded café, sipping it. The bitter liquid cools my anger, and slowly my breathing and heart rate come back to normal. I'm lost in some deep breathing when I hear the bell jingle over the door, announcing another customer. It's the woman from the crowd who was praying. My pulse starts to go back up. There are no seats left in the shop but the one next to me, and of course, she sits in it. As she does, she looks at me.

"I know you," she says. Her voice is as dry as the pink paper packets of sweetener she is pouring into her tea, dropping like dust to the bottom.

"I just have one of those faces," I say, not wanting the conversation.

"No, I know you. You were at the clinic. Awful place. Why would you go there?"

"There are lots of reasons women go there." Curt, not wanting to get into whatever this is.

"There's only one reason that matters." There is sadness in her voice, and she takes a long sip of her tea.

"You don't think my cancer screening matters?"

She takes a deep breath and looks me up and down.

"I suppose you're too old to be there to kill babies."

My anger flares hot. It's the "too old" and the "kill babies."

"I was too old when I did," she says, and I stop.

"When you did what?"

"In 1978, I walked out of the same building you did. And again in '80. There were no crowds on the way in then. I wish there were." Her voice breaks as she talks, and she sips tea through the straw. Beads of cold condensation drip off its bottom into the wet ring on the counter. I can tell she uses coasters at home, because she takes her shirtsleeve and wipes the water up before putting the tea back down.

It's funny how daydreams work, how little details pop up uninvited. They are conjured from our imaginations and give us a vivid picture of a person who doesn't exist. But this idea of a coaster and an older woman wiping a condensation ring off the table with a sleeve conjures my grandmother Nanny Honey. And just for an instant, she's with me, and she's with this woman sitting next to me, wiping my condensation rings off of her freshly polished table. The smell of lemon Pledge tickles the back of my memory, sweet and sour and slightly chemical, and I feel the humanity of this woman who wiped her ring. Like my grandmother.

This visit, this vision, it's especially unsettling since my grandmother is still with us.

And I see my companion as a little more human. A human who is maybe wrong about everything, but a human—and one who has just shared deep pain with me. And that pain deserves to be heard. "Tell me," I say to her, opening the door as wide as I am able, still bracing for the attack I know is coming.

"He forced me, you know, my husband. I didn't want to get pregnant. And I didn't want to have the abortions. I was going to be a nun until I met him." She looks out the window, watching the passersby, absently fingering her rosary and collecting herself to go on. "He was a force of nature."

"I'm a Catholic, too," I tell her.

She looks at me, skeptical. "How could you go into that awful place, knowing what happens there, if you're a Catholic?"

"Because what happens there saves lives."

"Ha! Saves lives. No, no, it takes them. And it ruins them." The rosary beads spin through her hands faster as she gets heated. "Every day, I know I'm damned for what I did. My husband, he's already in hell. Before long, I'll be stuck back with him again."

The beads stop, clacking on the black counter as she drops them.

"He might be," I tell her, trying to read the pain in her eyes, "but you won't. Even if you're right about everything, what God would let you suffer for being forced into making those decisions? All I want is for you to be able to have the choice, and the control over what happens to your body."

She sits silently for a moment. "God knows what God knows, and I know what the Bible says. 'Before I formed thee in the belly, I knew thee.'"

"I believe God loves us. And I believe that what Jeremiah wrote and abortion are unrelated. It's not a scriptural argument. It's about free will. You had no free will. Your husband took it from you. I want women to have free will," I tell her. "But more than that, I want to save lives.

"Let me tell you a story," I tell her. "My friend went into that building. She doesn't make much money, and they do regular gynecology exams. It's why I was there today. Her pap smear? It was irregular. No other signs. No other symptoms, but that pap smear led her to find out she had cervical cancer. It saved her life. What happens in that building saves lives."

"So you weigh your friend over all of the babies in there? The babies?"

"You and I are never going to agree that fetuses are babies.

If that's all we have to say about it, then we have nothing to talk about. I weigh my friend being here against the idea of her not being here. That's the only comparison that matters. Saving her? That's pro-life."

"They could do that without the abortions."

"Abortions save lives. They saved mine. I also had two abortions. I also didn't want to get pregnant, although I wasn't forced to. And I chose those abortions. I am terrified to think where my mental illness would have led me if I had been forced to carry those pregnancies to term and have children when I was so very much not ready to be a mother."

She looks at me sadly, judgment without fury.

I take out my wallet from the small purse I have with me. Inside are pictures of Milo and Bella. "These two babies, these joys of my life? They are here because I had those abortions. If I didn't, back when I was twenty, I never would have had them. They never would have lived. God knew them before he formed them in the belly, right? He knew."

She looked at the photos. "They are beautiful children. You met my son."

I looked at her, puzzled.

"He was outside, with me."

I see the man screaming at me in front of her. I see her flinch at the words he shouts at me. I see the hidden scars she carries from her husband and the legacy he pushed forward into their son, and I look at her with the same sadness with which she regarded me.

"He wants to be a good man. We all want to be good, most of us. I wish we were all better."

"So do I," I tell her. "So do I."

"We're never going to agree, you know." She says it with no heat and no regret. It's just a true statement.

"No," I say. "Probably not. But I think I understand you a little better now. And maybe you understand me."

She gathers her cup, empty save for a handful of melting ice cubes, and stands from her chair. She collects her rosary, wipes the counter again with her sleeve, shaking her head at the small ring left behind.

"I think maybe I do. I appreciated the talk. I'll pray for you," she says, and the door jingles as she makes her way out.

"And I'll pray for you," I say, watching her walk back down the street toward the clinic that saved my friend's life. And I do.

# Death in the Air

My daughter said to me in all her sass in the spring when the full force of the pandemic hit, "Mama, death is not so bad. You get to see all your animals and grandparents who have died already. You get to meet Martin Luther King Jr. and John Lennon." She was five at the time, and she said it with such sureness and confidence. Two weeks later, while we were homeschooling, working still, missing everyone, and juggling our sanity with laughter that would bleed into tears, our German shepherd passed away. Right at the peak of the coronavirus, we were forced to confront a mundane, everyday kind of death. The kind of death that punches you in the gut and leaves you stunned, surprised by an absence at every turn. It was in this surprise that I wrote the essay that follows, surrounded by death from afar and living with it in my house.

———

One custom I love that some who practice Judaism follow is that when a person dies, their body is guarded, watched over by another person from death until burial. It's called *shemira,* and it's sacred. I see so much beauty in this practice. In these moments of crossing the threshold between life and death, we need to be seen, to be protected, and to be accompanied into the unknown. The *shomer* or *shomeret*—the terms for men and women, respectively, who perform this vigil—may never have known the person who died. One New York synagogue's members volunteered to serve as virtual *shomrim* for Justice Ruth Bader Ginsburg when she died in 2020. There is an intimacy and connection that can only be experienced in death. After the burial, the mourners come together for a weeklong shiva. Mirrors are covered to keep their focus on the dead. At the core of both practices is such an important truth: The bereaved should never be alone in the hardest days after the loss of their loved one.

Across cultures and national boundaries, this is true. We mourn better together. At wakes and funerals and memorial services, we find our best selves. Here is where we are not afraid to cry in front of other people. There is no shame in needing or offering support. It is in these gatherings and in these connections that we begin to heal. They are where we find life when death would otherwise be bigger than anything we can bear. We come together in faith and love and sadness and darkness, and try to be the light for the people we love, in the memory of someone we loved.

As I write this, death is in the very air we breathe. We're sequestered in our homes, hiding from one another in a deeply fundamental way. We each could be an unknowing sleeper cell, and a simple handshake or even a wave hello from just a few feet away could be deadly. I'm very lucky that all of the humans in my family are safe and healthy so far, and we're able to stay distant from other people, largely together. I have my husband and my children and my dogs. But we've just lost my German shepherd Quixie. She was old, and her death lived in our minds long before it happened. Even so, we didn't expect it. She was here, and then one day she wouldn't get up. By the next day she was gone. I turn corners waiting for her. When my other dogs are playing in the backyard, I look for her trying to keep up with her younger siblings, only to re-member she's not out there anymore. Death exists without the virus. It's here in our homes. It's programmed into our cells, which have lysosomes specifically designed to break down and dissolve a cell when it can no longer function. Death is part of our very basic makeup.

This isn't unique to me. Pets or people, everyone's living it right now. Most of us have received the call at one time or another that one of our loved ones is dying or has died. The very first thing nearly all of us do in normal times is try very hard to find a way to be wherever that death is happening. And now, people are dying alone. Families are losing the very people who held them together, watching them die over Face-Time because there is too much risk in being there to hold their hands.

Even our death rituals have died.

There are no *shomrim*. There is no *shemira*. In many cases there are no timely burials or funerals held together with family and friends. The bereaved may meet via the internet, each mourner a square on a screen who is denied the absolutely essential physical presence, the actual shoulder on which to cry, the hand to squeeze, or the arms to collapse into in their grief. And I just don't know how we will bear this. I can't find my way past the idea of losing someone I love and not being able to observe the rituals of my Catholic faith, or to draw in the glow from others in that dark place.

When I turn off the light at night, this terror swirls in my head.

When the outbreak started, in the days before *social distancing* was a term we all knew, I read about a woman in Italy whose husband died in the house with her and nobody would come to claim the body. For more than two days, she had to stay alone in the house with the corpse of the man she'd spent her life with, waiting for the authorities to allow someone to break quarantine to help her. I can't imagine a more desperate or lonely situation. I don't know that I would survive it. But death is in the air. When we leave the spaces we know are safe, we could be breathing it in, taking it onto our skin and into our lungs. We are contaminated, and we contaminate each other. And so a new widow languished with her dead husband, waiting to see if his death foreshadowed her own.

In this contamination, the beautiful Islamic tradition of loved ones' ritually washing the body of the deceased takes on new importance and meaning. In washing the dead, lives are saved, as potential contagions are removed from the body of the person who passed. The physical purification becomes as important as the spiritual, cleansing the death off of the dead. I wonder if the Italian woman washed her husband's body. I wonder if it made her feel less alone.

Death is a physical process that has always been a part of the spiritual realm. We know exactly half of what happens when a person dies. Their breathing stops, and oxygen is no longer transferred through the tissues of the lungs into the blood vessels. The heart stops pumping, ceasing the circulation of blood through the body. Brain activity ceases, and we can no longer measure the electromagnetic waves that tell us "this person is alive." It is concrete. There is alive, and there is dead. But we don't know what happens to the spirit; death rituals, in many traditions, are designed to help not only the people left behind but also the soul of the dead person. It is part of the Catholic tradition that prayers for the dead help speed the transition from purgatory to heaven. Muslims gather together and pray for forgiveness of the dead. And while I am certain any loving god would forgive anyone overlooking these rituals in this specific time, I have nightmares about these abandoned souls waiting for us to help guide their way, and we have failed them.

It's more heartbreak in a time when too many hearts are already too broken.

But then there's the stupidity of some people who are inviting death by insisting on holding religious gatherings together when we *know* it is unsafe. Jerry Falwell Jr. allowed a new hot spot of infection to grow on the campus of Liberty University when he refused to close it despite nationwide closures of colleges and universities. Ammon Bundy, an anti-government activist who led an armed standoff against the federal government over grazing rights on public land, insists he will hold an Easter gathering in defiance of federal orders. Churches throughout America are shepherded by dangerous pastors who live in the arrogance that their demonstrations of faith are so pure that they will be protected from any sickness. I wonder if these preachers will perform the funerals of those in their congregations over Zoom.

As I walk outside in my yard, counting dogs and coming up one short, I smell barbecue. And sure enough, across the canyon a distant neighbor has a yard full of people, plates in hand, masks nowhere to be seen. The smoke-and-meat smell on the air carries all this way, and I wonder if the virus is carried with it. The wind picks up, and I see a quick flicker of bright orange flame briefly shoot up from the grill, sparking echoing laughter from a party that should not be happening. I see that party and the plume of thick, dark smoke from the grill that follows the flames, and it looks like a toxic factory spewing poison into my yard. Quickly I gather up Milo and Bella, call the dogs, and go inside.

There is death in the air.

I am now forced to contemplate my own mortality. What would I want if coronavirus claimed me? Part of me wants to just be mummified. Is that a thing? I'd like to be mummified while wearing a onesie. If that's not possible, I guess I would like to be cremated? Maybe? I don't know. I want whatever is going to be easiest for those I've left behind. By the way, this is why I had two children. So they can make these decisions together.

Death is something we all face, but we rarely face it in such high numbers from the same thing at the same time. And in this, I am taking a strange comfort, because if the people who are dying from this are forced to die alone, they are doing so together. If we the living can't be together on this side of death, perhaps the dead can be on the other. Maybe they are singing their hymns, saying their prayers for one another. They are their own funerals, joining together in a communion of souls, spiriting one another away to the beyond. I hope this is true. I hope there is something other than being wheeled into a rented refrigerated warehouse until it is deemed safe to dispose of the bodies.

Later in the day, I go back outside to let too few dogs out again. The party seems to have broken up, but I still hold my breath as long as I can. I'm like a kid holding her breath in the backseat until she has driven past the graveyard. But this time, there really is death in the air.

I can't wait to breathe without fear again.

# Defund the Police

I n September of 2020, an incident happened at my house
that required the intervention of my local police and sher-
iff's office. I want to tell the story as clearly and in as great a
degree of detail as I can, because what followed was a ridiculous series of lies from the right-wing press and its adherents
that not only displayed their wild distaste for reality but also
highlighted their willful ignorance and the depths of the racism behind their beliefs.

It started on a Sunday morning.

My husband and kids got up early. It was football season,
and as usual, they were getting ready to watch the Giants play.
I was still asleep, still recovering from my bout with COVID
from March. While I no longer felt like I was going to die, and
my blood oxygen levels were close to back to normal after the
terrifying lows of the illness, I was still dealing with the

exhaustion that was always present with the long-haul recovery I was experiencing. The immediate terror of "Am I going to die?" had been replaced with the constant, lower-level susurrus of "Will I always feel this bad?" swirling in my head. The plan of the day was to wake me up with a lot of coffee right before game time—ten A.M. on the West Coast—and then enjoy a few hours of my boys' pounding on the Chicago Bears. Neither the game nor the morning turned out as we hoped.

Before the coffee was even brewing, David came running into the room yelling, "Everybody into the theater, now!" My home has a small theater as an interior room, with some soundproofing and a door that locks. As we hustled downstairs, I was suddenly wide awake with the hyperalertness that comes with being jarred out of sleep into instant danger. Dave explained that he had gotten a call from a neighbor who had seen a man dressed entirely in black holding a long gun in the back of our property. The neighbor had called 911, which is exactly what anyone should do when they see a person with a gun on someone's property, and we went to shelter in place.

There is nothing more terrifying than an intruder in your home.

About a decade earlier, before my kids were born, a fan/stalker had come into my house. David wrestled him to the ground and pinned him there until the police arrived.

Afterward, he went out and bought guns. Since then, we have been a two-gun household.

"But Malano why do you get to keep you're guns when you want to take our guns away?" the trolls tweet all day long, bad spelling and all. Yeah, I'm not trying to take guns away, and that's a lie we'll get to in a minute, but first, I want to finish the story. Sit tight, trolls.

Once the kids, my parents (who were staying with us for the weekend), and I were safe but terrified in the theater, Dave went to get our guns. He then called 911 to both check on the arrival of the officers and update them that he was in our house with his guns, so that the officers would know he was armed when they arrived. During the entire ordeal, Dave stayed outside of the theater with the guns, and I stayed inside with the kids. We behaved as responsible citizens and as responsible gun owners.

When the police arrived, they told Dave they were treating it as an active-shooter situation. They had helicopters searching the area, a SWAT team, and a K-9 unit to search for the individual in question. Given the potential danger of a gunman to me, my family, and my neighbors, this seemed appropriate, and I suspect if this was the situation in your neighborhood with your family, you would feel the same. The police who responded could not have been kinder or more professional, and they made us feel safe and secure while they did their dangerous jobs. I'll always be grateful for the bravery and kindness they showed my family while they went about their work.

While I was huddling with my kids, trying to reassure them that we would be okay, that the police and their dad and I were all there to protect them, I started getting trolling tweets. An anonymous account, newly created during the crisis, tweeted very specific details about the police response, including the number of cars, the number of helicopters, and the presence of a K-9 unit. They used this to try to attack me for my calls to defund the police, implying—wildly incorrectly—that I am a hypocrite. I shared these screenshots with friends, and also with the FBI, as it seemed likely to me that these messages had to be from someone involved in creating this situation. There simply is no other way they could have obtained the level of detail they had. My home is not easy to get to. You can't just drive by it; it has a creek and a canyon behind it, and there's only one road in and out, which is gated. We moved here in part for the security after the stalker ended up in my home years ago.

A couple of hours later, an individual apparently called the police and identified themselves as the cause of the commotion. They claimed they were shooting squirrels with an air rifle. I have no way to know whether this was true, but I do know that no charges were filed in the end.

We spent the rest of the day trying to calm my kids, to

restore the sense of safety in their home that had been entirely shattered by either a careless trespasser or someone intentionally trying to scare my family due to our political beliefs. I think we have a word for that, don't we? Oh yeah, *terrorism.* My kids are traumatized, and will remain so. I'm traumatized, and it took weeks for my sleeping to get back to normal. But there is no way in hell I'm going to be silenced.

Two days later, I was interviewing Secretary Julián Castro for my podcast. He's a great guy, caring and personable and funny. During our conversation, my phone started exploding with notifications. This happens sometimes, and it's not often for a fun reason. I tried to put it out of mind while we finished our conversation, and then I learned what it was. A really terrible right-wing tabloid out of the United Kingdom, the *Daily Mail,* ran an article claiming, "EXCLUSIVE: 'Defund the police' activist Alyssa Milano calls 911 sparking massive police presence in her quiet California neighborhood claiming a gunman was on her property—but it was really a teen shooting at squirrels with an air gun." Full of lies, inaccuracies, and *photos of the police at my property,* this ridiculous and cowardly hit piece was designed to do one thing, and one thing only: undermine the "defund the police" argument by trying to paint me as someone who does not live her values. They, the ridiculous little propaganda blog *The Daily Wire,* and other right-wing outlets could not have been more wrong.

This incident—a potentially deadly situation caused by an unknown individual with a gun on someone else's property—is what the police are there for. They train to handle these situations. They have both the expertise to negotiate out of them and the authority to use force if necessary to protect the lives of innocent people. It's an unimaginably hard job just as that—putting oneself in danger in the protection of someone else. They are selfless in this, good and brave and doing what we *need* them to do. But the training we give them to do this work, which is lifesaving and so important, is exactly the opposite of the kind of training they need to respond to situations involving mental health crises, addiction issues, and nonviolent disputes that do not require an aggressive and armed response.

This is really important to note here: "Defund the police" does not mean "eliminate law enforcement." To me, it means that we should be dedicating resources in the ways they can be most effectively used. Police are not psychiatrists. They are not social workers. They are not referees. Like teachers, we're asking police to do things that they cannot do. We can't expect to train individuals to treat each situation like a potential threat and then be shocked when they respond that way. We need to ask the police to do less, so that they can focus on the already huge job we need them to do.

Take the case of Daniel Prude. Daniel was a forty-one-year-old father of five. It appears he had a recent history of mental illness and some issues with drug use. He'd also had a life full of tragedy, losing brothers and being home when a teenager died by suicide. He arrived in Rochester, New York, to visit his brother, where he had what some describe as a psychotic break, running outside in the cold New York March night without a shirt or shoes. His brother called 911, expecting the response would keep his brother safe.

Instead, the officers responded as if Daniel were an armed threat—because that's what officers do. By the time they arrived he was naked and allegedly claimed he had the coronavirus. They forced a spit hood over his head and placed him facedown on the street, and there is video of one officer pushing his face into the ground. He stopped breathing and was dead in a week.

He didn't need to be. No matter whether you blame the police, or the police training, or Daniel himself, you can't escape the reality that he was not a deadly threat and yet he met his death at the hands of police officers. The fear that each of us with any measure of common sense feels over COVID perhaps escalates violence in America, but it cannot be a justification for police murder. There are better ways, paths of de-escalation, that fear cuts off. And, with justification, police are afraid.

We can't ask our police to respond to both types of situations. We can't have them geared up to protect their own lives and expect them to be able to determine when someone is not a threat. Not in the way we do. If a trained mental health professional with some type of unarmed security showed up to this event, it's very likely Daniel Prude would be alive today. But we've put this burden on our police forces, and it is not working.

So why would we continue to do it? Why would we continue to allocate resources to the wrong people for the job instead of taking those same resources and investing them in the right people? Why would we overburden our police the way we do and ask them to do more than anyone should be asked to do? And why should our society be asked to bear the burden of the unnecessary deaths and incarcerations that result from our own failure to fix the problem that we ourselves created by asking the police to do far too much?

Of course, all of this overlooks one very true fact: If I were not a wealthy white woman, when police showed up at my home to find my armed husband, it is very likely things would have gone differently that day. This is not an attempt to say anything at all about the officers who responded to my home that day. As I've said before, and will always say, I am so grateful for their bravery and their professionalism. They could not have been kinder to me. But it doesn't erase the fact that there is racism built into every facet of our criminal justice system. We stop Black people more. We search Black people more. We arrest Black people more. We charge Black people more. We convict Black people more and give them longer sentences. The Stanford Open Policing Project has excellent data bearing this out, demonstrating clear bias in the way police interact with people of color. In Florida in 2016, Black motorists were about four times likelier to be searched if they were stopped by police. And before you scream, "Yeah, but that's FLORIDA," the same thing was true—by about the same proportion—in Massachusetts.

And we kill Black people more.

It's a simple fact. Numbers don't lie. The only choices you have are to believe that there is something inherently criminal about Black people or there is something inherently racist about our justice system. I do not believe there is anything at all inherently criminal about Black people. If you think differently, I don't want to know you. I don't want you as part of my nation. And I *especially* don't want you as part of law enforcement.

So yes, call 911 when someone shows up on your property with a gun. And yes, defund the police, so that they can do their jobs and we can save the lives of people who don't need a police response. Somebody tell the *Daily Mail* to learn a thing or two, write a retraction, and delete their whole thing.

And for you gun trolls: No, I am not trying to take away your guns—unless you're a domestic abuser, you're in a mental health crisis, you have a weapon of war, or you can't pass a background check. The vast majority of Americans—and of gun owners—agree with me.

And it's "your." You're dismissed.

# Essential

A new phrase entered the American lexicon when it became clear that the coronavirus was going to be more than just a few cases: *essential worker*. It became one of the most practically important terms in the country, defining who would go to work and who would stay home, but also who would get the vaccine and when. But it also became a philosophical term, forcing us to evaluate what—and who— mattered most in our communities.

We wrestled with realizations in America in 2020 about what is actually essential. We've been told *what* we can and cannot live without. We've been told *who* we can and cannot live without. We've been fed a glut of consumerism and a buffet of authority that fattened up the fattest calves while so many starved. We've been fed a line of shit.

Certainly, we know that grocery workers are essential.

This is absolutely true—the ability to access food for all Americans is a basic tenet of health and safety. We take it for granted that when we need to buy food, we'll be able to do so. We've even now been told that when there is a global pandemic, grocery workers—some of the lowest-paid employees in our nation—are so essential that they have to go to work to keep us safe, even at their own peril. I totally agree, access to food is essential.

But if it's so essential, why do nearly twenty-four million Americans live in "food deserts"? You know, the neighborhoods where people don't have easy access to fresh, healthy foods because there is no grocery store within a reasonable distance? Are vegetables not essential for the urban or rural poor? How the fuck can we decide something is so essential that the people who sell and stock it need to risk their lives for the rest of us while also not doing a damn thing to make sure those "essential" services are accessible to everyone? America, meet systemic racism. Meet systemic classism. If you've never had to worry about getting healthy food because you couldn't get to a grocery store that sold it? Meet your privilege.

One thing I know for sure: You can't call access to good, healthy food "essential" if you're trying to cut the SNAP budget—what we call "food stamps"—by hundreds of millions of dollars. Which is very much what the GOP has repeatedly tried to do. You can't allow people who can afford to both live in proximity to food and buy it to do so while simultaneously telling us we can't afford to take care of the people who can't. It's damned offensive.

Still, at least food *is* essential. We can all agree that we all need to eat. Food is one of the few things that truly are essential for human survival, and the pandemic should have been a wake-up call to America that we are failing to deliver that very basic need to a huge swath of Americans. Maybe it still will be. I hope so.

But what we all *should* be able to agree on? Guns are *not* truly essential.

Every year in America, six hundred women are shot to death by intimate partners. And during the pandemic, women across the nation were forced to stay at home with their abusers without even the respite of work or social engagements outside of the house. And because the NRA-backed, Republican-controlled Senate refused to allow a vote on the Violence Against Women Reauthorization Act because it contained provisions making it harder for domestic abusers to get guns, these women have even less protection and resources than they have had in decades.

Senate Republicans and many state governors chose the NRA and domestic abusers over their victims.

During the pandemic, people were scared. People were

angry. We saw it when we ventured out for essential items, especially food, and found empty shelves. We saw it when the person in the checkout line ahead of us coughed and everyone backed away. We felt it in our homes and saw it in the distant faces of our coworkers over remote meetings.

We saw it when the militias rose and plotted to kidnap and execute my friend Gretchen Whitmer, the governor of Michigan. We saw it in the spittle-faced Proud Boys losing their shit over Black Americans exercising free speech. We saw it in the Queen of the Karens and her pink-shirted husband pointing their guns at each other and a crowd of peaceful Black Lives Matter protesters marching past their property. And we've seen it in the nonstop onslaught of gun deaths, which has not diminished despite the fact that we didn't *go* anywhere during the pandemic.

And then there is what happens in the home. Nearly two out of three of the gun deaths in America are self-inflicted. Now, with people isolated from their support systems and medical professionals, many of them facing job loss or other economic uncertainty, we know we are likely to see a rise in deaths by suicide. There are already instances of this happening, and it will only get worse.

FBI data shows that more than three million additional guns were sold in 2020 than would have been expected in a "normal" year, driven by coronavirus fears. In a letter to FBI director Chris Wray, Senators Ed Markey, Chris Murphy, and Richard Blumenthal warned that this surge could overwhelm the background check system. Because federal law allows gun sales to proceed after seventy-two hours whether or not the check has been completed, this will undoubtedly put guns in the hands of domestic abusers, violent felons, and other people not legally allowed to have guns, endangering each of us.

It's not just the immediate risk of physical violence, however, although this is a pressing and real concern. This move, the refusal to reauthorize the Violence Against Women Act when it expired in 2019 following gun-industry lobbying, erodes the fundamental essence of our government. Government exists solely to provide for the welfare of its citizenry. Instead, these politicians have done the exact opposite: put us all at greater risk to grovel at the feet of the gun lobby.

Never once has the ability to shoot someone been essential.

Our priorities are so broken.

I have a friend who is a teacher in the New York City public schools. If food is the most essential need our society has, the education of our children has to be close behind. We've called our teachers heroes, and rightfully so, for learning how to adapt and teach our children in entirely new ways on the fly. We've learned as parents, when we've had to step in, just how hard that job is and how ill equipped we are to be teachers. We have seen that my friend and the millions of teachers like her are truly essential.

Why did our cities not see this? Or if they did, why did they continue to place our teachers at risk by sending them unsafely into classrooms? Some cities, like Chicago, even tried to force teachers who were caretakers of at-risk people into the classroom. My friend had to go and teach in a classroom in a school that failed its COVID safety checks. Wearing a mask and a face shield, she was required to go into a classroom and teach. But get this: She did not teach the kids in her own classroom. There were kids there in her classroom, but not *her* students. She was teaching other kids in different classrooms, learning via their computers. The kids in her classroom? They were trying to learn from their teachers, who were *also* in the building, but in different classrooms. Every kid had teachers in their room, but not their own teacher. And to put the icing on the cake? There was a second teacher in the classroom, six feet away from my friend. This teacher was also teaching their students, who were in different classrooms with different teachers.

This shitshow is such a nightmare that Betsy DeVos must have been the person who planned it.

Listen, I get that schools perform an outsized function in our society. They are a point of contact for nearly all families in a community, and that makes them easy distribution points for services: food services, health services, social services. Things that teachers and schools were not designed to provide, but they have been called on to do so regardless— because it's the easiest way to deliver these services. But here's the thing: If something is essential, we do it even when it's not easy. When it's not convenient. When it's not cheap. Each of these services schools provide is essential—but they are not part of the essential functions of the schools. We are among the wealthiest nations ever to sit on the face of the Earth, and we can't figure out how to feed our kids if they can't come to school? We can't figure out how to get them health screenings? Psychological counseling, safe shelter, or the internet access they need to learn or study? I mean, Jeff Bezos alone is worth nearly $200 billion. The annual income for a family of four must be under $33,500 to qualify for free school lunches. That family would have to work for nearly six million years without spending a penny to accrue the wealth Bezos already holds. Donald Trump reported assets worth more than $1.4 billion, and yet paid only $750 in federal taxes in 2017.

And we can't figure out how to deliver these essential services to our kids.

Flint still doesn't have clean water. More than two million people in America don't have access to safe, clean running water. *Water.* Is there anything more essential? And another nearly six million live in communities where PFA

ALYSSA MILANO

contaminant levels in the water exceed EPA limits. And guess who those two million are? Urban people of color. The rural poor. Tribal communities. The people we overlook every single damn time something we call *essential* is threatened for those of us with the most privilege. Do you think if Park Avenue couldn't turn on the tap, the federal government wouldn't do something about it?

I don't think we know what *essential* means.

Here's what it means to me:

Every night before I go to bed, I kiss Milo and Bella good night, and I sleep knowing they will be safe and fed in the morning. That is essential for me, and it is essential for every family. I can afford the medications I need to manage my generalized anxiety disorder, and I know that if I have a spike in my symptoms, I will be able to receive top-notch medical care wherever I am in the country because I can afford it. This is essential and must be true for every person. I know that I can flip the light switch and the lights will come on. I know that I can turn on the stove and the gas will come on. I know that I can turn up the thermostat and the heat will come on, and I know that each of these things will happen in a home I am not at risk of losing because I can't afford it. This is essential and must be essential for every person.

I know that I can vote, and that my vote will be counted,

and that I won't have to wait in line for seven hours to cast it on machines that were outdated twenty years ago. This must be essential for every person.

I know that if I get pulled over for speeding, I won't be shot by a police officer. This must be essential for every person.

I know that my parents, who are in their seventies, are safe. I know that as they age, their income and their medical care and their housing will be safe, because I can afford it. This must be true for every person.

In 2020, we talked so much about what *essential* means, but we almost never lived it. Essential is not conditional. It is not a function of affordability. *Essential* means something we *cannot do without.* The people we lost to COVID were essential to us. We are broken, different than we were before they died. Their absence creates a food desert of the soul. We are starving in their loss.

It is time to start living our values around the things that are essential. The things that are part of our essence. The things we cannot live without. We need to extend those values to everyone. The security I feel in my privilege should be the security everyone feels in America. Home. Food. Safety. Shelter. Water. It's the first level of Maslow's hierarchy of needs, and we're meeting it for only some of our people? If we can't meet this for the people who live in America, we are a failed nation with so many generations of failed leadership on critical issues of poverty and racial justice that we can't even see how to get it right.

But we can start.

A government that meets the needs of *all* of its people, not just the white and wealthy? That's the new essential.

# The Olive Branch

*Resolve me, strangers, whence, and what you are; Your business*
*here; and bring you peace or war?*
                                    —PALLAS TO AENEAS, *Aeneid,* book 8

P allas, son of Evander, son of Hermes, stood on the shore
   with a javelin in hand, facing the fleet of the Trojans.
The air was thick with the smoke of the day's offerings to Her-
cules and heavy with fear at the approach of the strange ships
in the middle of the day. This was a time of war, of great
conflict, and unexpected ships filled with soldiers were not a
welcome sight. Thinking his city was being invaded, he
stood ready for combat and challenged Aeneas to state his
purpose.

Aeneas came ashore, bearing an olive branch extended in
peace, and the two rejoiced in new friendship. They had been
at the brink, at the very precipice of terrible war, and with a
stick laden with a few morsels of fruit, that war was avoided.
The branch stretched from the hand of Aeneas on one side

and replaced the javelin in the hand of Pallas on the other, releasing the tension of impending battle. Peace reigned.

This is the origin of extending an olive branch. I always thought it came from Genesis, in which a dove comes to Noah carrying an olive branch, signaling the end of the Great Flood. And while that is a moment of revelation and peace and salvation—much like the moment Aeneas and Pallas found on the shores of Evander's city—it lacks a critical component of the actual original story: An olive branch must be accepted, and the peace it symbolizes must be honored. The possibility of betrayal exists in an offer of peace. There is risk in the offer and risk in the acceptance. And who knew this better than the Trojans?

We know the story of the Trojan Horse from earlier in Virgil's *Aeneid*. Following a decade-long siege, the Greeks built a giant wooden horse, left it on the shores of Troy, and sailed away. Thinking they'd achieved a great victory, the Trojans wheeled the horse into the city as a symbol of the end of the conflict. However, it was crammed full of Greek warriors who, as the residents of Troy slept through their first peaceful night in years, snuck out and sacked the city. It can be dangerous to offer peace, and it can be dangerous to accept peace.

After the 2020 election was decided, I sent out a tweet. Here's what it said: "I'd like to extend an olive branch to Trump supporters. I am ready to move #ForwardTogether. There's so much work to do to heal the nation. Let's be a part of the solution and not add to the problems we face. My comments are open. Please reply with #ForwardTogether. ♡" Apparently the left thought this meant I was building a shrine to Trump, and the right thought this meant that they could continue to behave in despicable, deplorable ways and I was just going to go along with it.

Bullshit.

We live in a world where Rush Limbaugh called openly for civil war, saying there is no place for "peaceful coexistence." Limbaugh didn't have to worry about coexisting with anything for long given his terminal lung cancer diagnosis near the end of the Trump regime, but he seemed pretty content with throwing firebombs during his ignominious stroll out the door. The rest of us, though, at least the ones who survived Trump and McConnell's COVID failures, will be here holding the pieces now that Limbaugh's at the eternal barbecue. But I'm not content to watch the fire he incited burn, and neither should you be. We're on the precipice, each of us in Aeneas's ship, and each of us Pallas on the shore, holding a javelin as the smoke of the offerings fills the sky. One false move now, and it can all go south. It almost did all go south on January 6, when hordes of domestic terrorists stormed the United States Capitol in a futile attempt to thwart a democratic election.

And we've seen it go south before. Last time, it led to many of the deadliest days in American history. Antietam. Gettysburg. Sherman burning Georgia as he chased the last remnants of the Confederacy. Then we had a cause—the South demanded slavery, and the North didn't want the expansion of slavery. There were few heroes in that fight, few true idealists about freedom—but it was an evil that needed to be lanced, a war that was altogether necessary to end a stain that may never otherwise wash out of the American fabric.

There are grave injustices in America today. The wealthiest people in our country hoard our nation's wealth, actively keeping so many people so very poor. Institutionalized racism is no secret, and yet it continues to fester and flare, killing and incarcerating and impoverishing people of color while gripping the reins of power with its albino-white knuckles. The very idea that we're even having an argument over whether everyone should have equal access to high-quality health care that is affordable and never creates a wrenching choice between medicine and rent is fucking soul-crushing. Sexual discrimination piles onto sexual assaults to keep women out of power and unsafe. Immigrants cannot find safety here in our land, citizens cannot find clean air and water. Bigoted members of Congress think the most important thing they can work on is filing legislation discriminating against trans athletes. Oh yes, there are grave injustices.

But these injustices are not terminal. Unlike the cowards

who call for civil war, unlike complete morons like Allen West—a far-right politician formerly of Florida and now chair of the Texas GOP—who call for secession, I believe the Union is salvageable and worth fighting for. I believe we have to find a way to move forward together even while addressing the ills of the past or they will just keep extending out into the future for generation after generation. I think we have to look to the surrender of Robert E. Lee, whose legend says he was allowed to keep his sword while ending the bloodiest war in American history. A gesture of honor from the winner to the loser, a nod to the future, and an olive branch extended.

Now, if Robert E. Lee had taken that sword and run Grant through, the fact that an olive branch had been extended would not have kept the assembled Union troops from shooting him dead and wiping his surrendered army off the face of the earth. The extension of a peace offering is not permanent and not a license for continued bad behavior. Which is why I can't help but laugh at the people on the right who bleated, "I THOUGHT YOU OFFERED AN OLIVE BRANCH, MILANO," when I continued to call out the bullshit that Trump and Ted Cruz and Rudy Giuliani and so many others shoveled down the throats of America in the days after the 2020 election. My olive branch did not give them permission to continue to abuse the nation. Neither did it require silence from me.

I will not be silent. And I will hold to account those who are not willing to accept a peace offering every single time. Do not mistake an olive branch for a white flag. It's extended from a place of power, from the hand of the victor to the hand of the vanquished. Those who refuse to accept it still lost, but the losing will be a lot more painful than it needs to be. Instead of finding commonality and ways to work together, we will bulldoze right over those who would perpetuate the things that are keeping America sick. We'll burn every bridge if that is what it takes for the failed institutions to come tumbling down. Make no mistake about that.

But I don't want to burn. I want to build. I'd rather be the architect of peace instead of performing a controlled burn.

Olive groves can't grow in a place of war. Each tree takes years and years to produce fruit. It takes careful attention, healthy air, clean water, and clean soil. It takes skilled hands tending to it, carefully pruning and making sure it has just the right environment in which to grow. Too much war, too much destruction, and there won't be olive branches to extend anymore. There will be no peace offerings, because we will have lost the symbols of peace. We will have forgotten how to be peaceful, how to extend a hand that isn't holding a javelin, how to keep from throwing it when strangers appear in their ships at midday. And with that, we'll be lost.

So my olive branch remains extended. The fruit is withering, and the leaves are drying out. My arm is getting tired, and the long night is about to fall. Isn't there anybody with enough vision, courage, empathy, and humility on the other side to take it before it's too late?

I hope there is.

# Amendments

*The Congress, whenever two thirds of both houses shall deem it necessary, shall propose amendments to this Constitution, or, on the application of the legislatures of two thirds of the several states, shall call a convention for proposing amendments, which, in either case, shall be valid to all intents and purposes, as part of this Constitution . . .*

—UNITED STATES CONSTITUTION, Article V

To err is human. The Framers knew it. They knew that they, in their own time, could not foresee their own biases and failures or the needs of the world to come. This was their greatest gift to us—that instead of throwing the nation away when its challenges exceed the framework in which we exist, we can change that framework to meet those challenges.

The framework needs some changing.

Women do not exist in the Constitution. Seriously, read it. We're not in there. Men are in there. Landowning men are in there. Alcohol is in there. As I've mentioned earlier, where soldiers can and cannot be quartered is in there. How long the Framers had to wait before amending the Constitution around the slave trade is in there. Women? Not so much.

It's the biggest still-unamended black eye in our national government. Women just are not in there, in any way. And before you start yelling, "But, Alyssa, the Fourteenth Amendment guarantees everyone equal protection under the law," riddle me this: If the Fourteenth Amendment really did that, why did we need a Nineteenth Amendment to give women the right to vote? Hint: It's because women don't exist in the Constitution. We're left to the whims of a politically weaponized Supreme Court, regressive state legislatures, and a Congress too weak to do a damn thing anymore. "Surely," said the late Supreme Court justice Antonin Scalia, "the Constitution does not require discrimination on the basis of sex. The only issue is whether it prohibits it. It doesn't."

Now, back in the 1970s, Congress passed the Equal Rights Amendment through the House and the Senate by clearing the high constitutional bar of a two-thirds approval in both houses and sent it to the states for ratification. The approval of thirty-eight states was needed to enact it. And in 2020, Virginia *finally* became the thirty-eighth state to do so. The ERA *should* be law now. It should be in the Constitution. Women should have full protection in America's founding document, sending a strong message at home and around the world that America will not tolerate discrimination based on sex. It's so important—how can America be a world leader on equality when we don't have it at home? How can we tell nations like Saudi Arabia that they need to treat women fairly and equally when we don't need to do so here in America? We have no moral ground to stand on and no incentive for the rest of the world to act in the best interest of the women who live in their nations.

So why isn't the ERA in the Constitution if thirty-eight states have ratified it? Because Congress put a poison pill in the original bill—an arbitrary deadline that gave states a limited time frame to pass the law, which expired in the 1980s. The Constitution has no such mandate. The last time the Constitution was amended, back in 1992, we enacted the Twenty-Seventh Amendment, which placed modest restrictions on congressional pay. Know when that was sent to the states for ratification? Seventeen eighty-nine—the year the Constitution was first adopted. It took more than two hundred years to enact it. So why is the ERA limited to fifty?

Patriarchy, that's why.

Congress can fix this. There have been bills put forth in Congress after Congress to remove this useless and unnecessary deadline and allow the will of the people to match the vision of the Framers. But there has never been a Congress with the courage or integrity to do so. I honestly can't even tell you why this is controversial. How can someone think granting women equal protection under the law will hurt us? Ninety-four percent of Americans support the ERA. The remaining 6 percent are apparently all the men in Congress standing in the way of progress. This needs to change, and it needs to change now.

But the ERA is not the only change we need to make to our Constitution. Every four years, we watch as four or five states decide who will preside over America. Twice in this century, the people voted for a candidate who did not assume the office of the presidency because of the Electoral College. It is a terrible and outdated relic of slavery—enacted to ensure the slave states, which had smaller voting (white) populations than their Northern counterparts, were able to maintain their power by counting (part) of their slaves toward their population. It continues to disenfranchise millions of voters of color in favor of thousands of white voters, and it needs to go.

North Dakota gets three electoral votes. It has a population of 762,000, or 254,000 people per elector. Eighty-seven percent of those voters are white. California, which is far more diverse, has a population of 39.5 million that is 59 percent white. It gets fifty-five electoral votes, or 718,000 people per elector. A vote in North Dakota is almost three times more powerful than a vote in California when it comes to selecting the president. This is fucking insane. I love you, North Dakota, but there is no reason at all your votes should count more than someone in South Central Los Angeles. None. Zippo.

"But, Malissa Alano," some of you will scream, "if we don't have an electoral college, the states on the coasts will decide every election." No, the *people* will decide every election. One person, one vote—and those votes all mean the same thing. Think of it this way: In the 2020 election, about 30 percent of voters in Massachusetts voted for Donald Trump. Why, I have no fucking clue, but they did. But every single one of that state's electoral votes went to Joe Biden. The votes of those 30 percent of people—from a coastal state—very literally did not matter when it came to selecting who would or would not be the next president. They were erased by the Electoral College. In a world where the presidency is selected as it should be, by the people, those 1.15 million Trump votes in Massachusetts would have been added to the 4.8 million Trump votes in California that were also erased. Those votes would have had a chance at mattering, whereas in our current system, they just disappear.

There is a plan to effectively remove the significance of the Electoral College, called the National Popular Vote Interstate Compact. It is an agreement between states that, when sufficient states join the compact and thus represent a majority of Electoral College votes, every state in the compact would allocate all of their electors to the winner of the national popular vote. It's a brilliant strategy, effectively giving every voter the same say in the selection of the president and vice president and rendering the Electoral College moot. It's something every state should adopt, but as of this writing it is still a few states short of being enacted. It includes the states you might expect—like New York and California, whose electoral power is diminished by the Electoral College—but also small states like Vermont and Rhode Island, whose power is increased by it.

The problem with doing it this way, however, is the Supreme Court.

I, and legal experts around the country, strongly believe this is a constitutional way to reflect the will of the people. The Tenth Amendment makes this pretty clear, giving any powers not specifically reserved for the federal government in the Constitution to the states. But the right has weaponized the Supreme Court, creating a radical-right majority accountable only to their own bigoted and biased whims. I fear this new court will have less regard for the Constitution and great regard for their own warped ideology. I fear they will throw the Interstate Compact out on its ear, allowing a tyranny of the minority to continue to rule over the will of the people.

So we must make this happen. We need an amendment to abolish the Electoral College permanently. We need to be better than the will of the slave states in 1789. And speaking of 1789, I sure wish they had been more specific about that whole "well-regulated militia" thing. See, I'm a supporter of the Second Amendment. I've had creeps show up at my home. You can be damn sure if you show up as a threat to my family, my husband or I will shoot you. But we don't want to. We don't want them to be able to shoot us, either. It's not what the Second Amendment is for, just what it's been perverted to mean. Let me explain.

Back in the 1780s, a "well-regulated militia" meant a "functioning militia." Does anyone think, even a little bit, that the epidemic of gun violence today is emblematic of a functioning militia? The only people who seriously think differently are the roving bands of militias that threatened our government by plotting to kidnap governors and assaulted the Capitol. The Framers intended for there to be only a small standing federal army and needed the ability to call upon the states to reinforce that army in a time of crisis. They did not mean that George Zimmerman could murder Trayvon Martin and get away with it.

Hundreds of years of law backs this up. The militia was clearly codified by a series of Militia Acts, the most recent one in 1903. Do you know how those laws defined the militia? As the National Guard. The militia is a series of state-managed militaries that can be federalized in a time of crisis by order of the president. Now, that act also created an inactive militia,

but that was very specific and did not include the vast majority of Americans. Rather, it included men between the ages
of seventeen and forty-five. Not women, not middle-aged
men. Not senior citizens. Not children. Men of military age.
That's it.

From the time the Constitution was written to the early
part of this century, there was no presumption of an individual right to own a gun. None. This was clear, and defined, and
acted upon, right up until the right-wing Supreme Court
threw out those centuries of precedent in handing the NRA
and the funeral industry a cash boon in 2008 in *District of Co-
lumbia v. Heller.* This sweeping, shortsighted, and deadly rul-
ing will continue to plague America until we fix it.

I am not proposing we do away with the right to bear arms.
I am proposing we update the Second Amendment to reflect
the challenges we face today. The Framers could not have
foreseen the massacres in our schools and streets. They could
not have foreseen the rogue bands of traitors passing themselves off as patriots while threatening the government itself.
They could not have foreseen the dark night in Aurora, Colo-
rado, when a nightmare burst into a movie theater and filled it
with bullets and death.

We need to change. We need to adapt. We need to evolve.

And we have the platform to do these things. We have
amendments, the gift of humility the Framers gave us. We

have the power to see where things are going wrong and set them right. The question, then, is, do we have the courage? Do we have the wisdom? Do we have the will to take the power the Framers handed to us and wield it to shape a future we all deserve? The jury is out on that one. We don't have that wisdom in the majority of our leaders right now. We have cowards like Mitch McConnell instead. We have the anti-American sentiment of the gerrymandering Republicans and the special interests they represent. We have the least visionary, least functional Supreme Court in our lifetimes, and more challenges than we can carry.

We have our work cut out for us.

But I believe. I believe we can change. Our Framers believed we could change. And our future demands it of us.

# Taking Care of One Another

Why do governments exist? What's the point? I know there are a lot of people out there who think they shouldn't—that government, if it exists at all, should be a bare-bones operation that maintains the ability to keep the lights on at a national level. And maybe has a giant arsenal of nukes to throw at other nations if they decide to come poking around. Well, they couldn't be more wrong. Government exists to make sure society continues to function. And societies work by pooling our strengths to cover our weaknesses. Society exists as a way to take care of one another, and it follows that governments are there to protect our ability to take care of one another.

That's why governments exist. They are, in their pure form, a way for us to protect one another from the darkness of night, when things are dangerous and when we would not be safe alone. Government helps us take our young, our vulnerable, our neediest, and bring them into the center, where those of us best able to survive the night stand guard.

Not too long ago I was watching a nature documentary on pack animals. So many of the behaviors were fascinating. Some, as predators drew near, brought the old and the sick and the young and the weak into the middle of the pack while those who were stronger, whose turn it was to defend, who had the *resources* to protect those who could not protect themselves, formed the perimeter. Yes, there was some risk to them. Yes, some sacrifices were made. But they knew instinctively that protecting the past and the future made them stronger as a group. That the risk they assumed, that the sacrifice they offered, was for a greater good. But mostly, they weren't in danger, because the show of strength, the circle of protection by the strongest, was more than a solo predator could overcome.

In other groups, it was the most vulnerable who moved around the most frequently, placing themselves between the strongest and danger. Sometimes members of the pack took turns on the inside and outside, making sure no single individual was more at risk than any other single individual. While the tactics and the methods varied from species to species, from habitat to habitat, the outcome was the same: When groups worked together and protected one another, they were more successful in driving off dangers, in warding off threats, and in keeping everyone alive.

This is what our government is supposed to do. This is why we as a people band together, why we pay taxes, why we live in communities. This is why we have laws and how we have freedoms. We enter into a shared responsibility to one another, a societal contract, a commitment to *take care of one another*. I pay taxes so that your roads are paved just like mine. I pay taxes so that you can have access to health care. You pay taxes so that the food I buy at the grocery store has been inspected and deemed safe. None of us individually can do each of these things. We are bound by the larger community and our better selves.

And it's why it pisses me off so much to see so little voter participation and so many screaming about paying taxes. On both ends, it's an expression of irresponsibility, a willful violation of that social contract. Oh, many of these people still take. They benefit from the contract—their weaknesses are covered just fine. But they have no commitment to give. Selfishness has become the American way, for far too many of us.

Now, I know—I *know*—that there are reasons many voters are disenfranchised. There has been a decades-long campaign by the Republicans to make it hard for people of color to vote. For people in cities to vote. For young people to vote. And for those votes to be counted. It's a feature of their electoral strategy, and it sucks. And before that, before the 1960s, the Democrats did the same. For decades, my party worked hard to make sure Black people especially could not vote, and it is their deepest shame. The difference is that every Democrat I know is committed to trying to fix it. But the Republicans are trying to duplicate it.

But that does not account for the rest of the people who do not vote. When we look at the popular vote as a percentage of our population, there were two giant leaps in our history: The first was just after 1870, when the Fifteenth Amendment gave Black Americans the right to vote. Then, we went from about 15 percent turnout to about 20 percent turnout among eligible voters. Pretty weak, but that's a better than 30 percent increase over a few years. The next big leap? Women's suffrage. In the two decades after women were given the right to vote, turnout went from about 16 percent to nearly 40 percent. Women and people of color showed up. But voting as a percentage of the population has never broken 50 percent, and voting among eligible voters has never once exceeded 60 percent in my lifetime. That sucks.

It's disheartening that so many people care so little for the people in their neighborhoods, their states, their nation. It crushes me that so many people look around and complain—because, let's be honest, all of us complain about how things are going in America and many of us sit back and do nothing about it. And it pisses me off that so many of these people have the means, the access, the information, and the ability to vote—to make an affirmative statement that says "I care about what happens to the people in my society"—and instead make a conscious choice to do nothing. How disgusting is that? To be offered the choice to care, and to affirmatively reject it? Shame on each of you reading this who makes that choice. Do better.

But as angry as I am at the people who don't vote, I'm even angrier at those of us who complain about taxes, who do everything they can to avoid paying taxes, and who work to make sure tax money doesn't go to those who need it most. People who claim a net worth of billions and pay taxes of $750, for example. People who have the money to have capital gains, and who also have the audacity to think this income should somehow be less taxable than the honest wages of a dishwasher making ten dollars an hour. The entitled investor, the bully billionaire, the selfish beneficiary of a large inheritance. The entitled elite.

Nearly universally, these are people who have never known hardship. These are people who grew up in wealth and whose idea of austerity means vacationing on this continent instead of on another. These are people who make their wealth on the backs of the hard work of others—others who often pay higher tax rates than they themselves do, at much lower incomes—and who feel entitled to every last benefit they get while deriding those who need help. They sicken me, and the lawmakers who make sure they are first at the trough sicken me even more.

These people will scurry to the center of the pack every time a predator is near. They buy their way out of drafts. On the rare occasions when they get caught for their crimes, they rarely receive prison sentences, and when they do they are slaps on the wrist. They hoard wealth and have the cynical audacity to make charitable contributions *for the tax deductions*. More than almost anything, this wealth gap—this *caring* gap—is killing our society. Predators are circling because they can smell the weakness. They can see the pack starving because these few take all of the best resources, dole out a few scraps to those who keep them safe, and demand protections for it.

It's time to make these people do their time on the fringes.

Before the pandemic, food pantries were struggling. In every grocery store, there are bins for donations and signs listing what they need. In a country where more than 30 percent of the food supply is wasted, dented cans fill the bins. We have the capacity to end hunger not just domestically but close to globally. We have more than eight hundred billionaires here, nearly half of the world's population of the uber-rich. Combined, they have a net worth of more than three trillion.

Three. Trillion. Do you think they could get by on two trillion? Could we maybe tax a trillion out of them to, I dunno, cure cancer? Feed every hungry family in the nation? End homelessness? Totally eliminate two-thirds of American student debt?

Despite the mythology, there is no such thing as a self-made billionaire. It doesn't exist. These financial logjams are created by an army of workers supporting the individual at the top. I guarantee you none of those workers are billionaires. Few of them are millionaires. And yet, they are the ones the billionaire is standing on, fighting like hell to keep the hands of their employees off of their pie. It is anti-American. It is antihuman. And it shows how little they are interested in being part of a society that takes care of one another.

The people who don't vote, the people who don't share the wealth, the people who dodge taxes? They are putting us in danger. They are existential threats to our pack. They are allowing the dangers of the night to creep closer and steal away our young, our elders, our future. The lawmakers who enable them are the collaborators, helping the wealthiest and hoping that some table scraps will be thrown into their campaign troughs. We won't survive it—the pack will fail, and we'll be forced to scurry alone in the darkness, weaker and colder and hungrier because of their selfishness.

We need to start taking care of one another.

# Reconciliation

*This process is not about pillorying. It's actually about getting to the truth, so we can heal.*
—Archbishop Desmond Tutu, chair, Truth and Reconciliation Commission, South Africa

In apartheid South Africa, grave injustice ruled every moment of every day. It was an evil on the scale of segregation in America, and echoes of that evil still ripple across the African continent. And while the violence and damage done by apartheid, the atrocities committed against Black South Africans by a racist, vile, and hateful regime—and by some Black South Africans in response to the evils of that regime as well—may never be set right, the efforts to heal the scars of that violence are even greater and more profound. While not perfect, the demonstrations of remorse, the statements of truth, the desire to heal individually and collectively, and the saintly granting of forgiveness by those who were wronged are among the most powerful things I have observed.

Let me start with a story: Amy Biehl was murdered.

She was a young, white American student, a great admirer of Nelson Mandela. She was a Fulbright scholar, a brilliant young woman visiting South Africa to study. She was not part of the South African political class and was opposed to apartheid. One day she was driving friends home when there was political unrest and violence in a township just outside of Cape Town. She was dragged from her car, beaten, and stabbed to death. It was a brutal act, full of violence and rage and directed at the wrong person. She was a victim of generations of racial subjugation, and the rage that subjugation engendered.

Eric Taylor was a white South African police officer. During apartheid, he took part in the horrific killing and burning of four anti-apartheid activists now called the "Cradock Four." These young men were driving and were stopped at a police barricade by six officers. Later that night, two of their badly beaten bodies were found burned nearby. The other two were not found for days, and it is likely they were interrogated and tortured by police—including Taylor. Years later, Taylor says, he saw the American film *Mississippi Burning*. This set him on a path to a new way of thinking, and a desire to come forward and speak about what happened and his role in it.

Each of these cases was brought before the Truth and Reconciliation Commission, chaired by Archbishop Desmond Tutu, in the aftermath of the fall of apartheid and the end of the Afrikaner government in Cape Town in the early 1990s.

These commissions were powerful tribunals where victims of gross human rights violations could give testimony about their experiences, and perpetrators of violence and abuses could come forward to confess their crimes and seek amnesty. These commissions required those seeking amnesty to make a full and detailed confession of their crimes, express and *feel* remorse, and ask their victims—or their families—for forgiveness.

Imagine the weight of that moment. Amy Biehl's killers had to tell her family what happened—what they did—and beg their forgiveness for it. Eric Taylor had to tell the wives of his victims what he did—specifically—and beg their forgiveness. They had to experience the pain they caused, they had to confront it, they had to apologize for it, and they had to ask for forgiveness that was not always granted. It restored to the victims some power, and to the confessors some humanity. It found the *truth* of what happened, and it fostered real and important change in so many of those who participated in it on both sides.

Amy Biehl's parents forgave her killers, and they were granted amnesty. The wives of Eric Taylor's victims did not forgive him, and he was not granted amnesty. But in both instances, people on either side of terrible violence, horrible crimes, and a racial structure of injustice that created the circumstances that drove each side to enmity came together to attempt to reconcile. There was a forced introspection, a probing of the hurts caused and the hurts received, and a measuring of those hurts against forgiveness. Sometimes the hurts were too large, the imbalance not able to be reconciled. This is okay—not every crime can be forgiven, and there can be healing in justice. Others were able to find healing in the gift of forgiveness. But in each of these instances, the person who did the wrong came forward and said, "I did this. I am so sorry for the hurt I caused you and your family. Can you forgive me?"

Now, this was not a perfect fix. This did not end all anger or resentment in South Africa. It did not bring the dead back to life, nor did it fix all of that nation's woes. Anger and resentment linger to this day. But what it did do—what it made possible—was create a path back from the brink for those most harmed by apartheid and those who did the harm. It found a way for people who still had to live in the same country together after this disgusting and deadly system of oppression fell to coexist. It offered a path to healing, which is so much more than what was there before the commissions.

We need Truth and Reconciliation Commissions here in America.

I've thought about this so often since my #MeToo tweet went viral a few years back. The men who did these things are *still here*. For many of them, their actions did not rise to the level of life in prison, and many men were acting in the way they were raised to. I say this *not* to absolve them—I can't absolve men who did not assault me, and I don't know if I can absolve the men who *did* assault me. I have rage still deep in my soul over what happened to me. But I also know that these men will never go to jail for what they did. There will not be justice. There could be poetic justice—I could name them and ruin their careers—but would that help? They will still be there.

But what if they had to sit in a room across a table from me and say out loud what they did, with witnesses looking on? What if there was a public record of their tribunal? What if they had to feel remorse and to demonstrate that remorse *to me*? What if they had to humble themselves in front of a commissioner and ask me to forgive them? I know one thing that would certainly come from that: vindication. No longer would I have to worry about saying "This happened" and being shouted down by those who want to silence victims of sexual trauma.

But another thing it would offer, another thing it would force, would be a vast education of men. Men who had to look into the faces of their victims and admit what they did, and that it was wrong. It would create a path back from patriarchy, from causing sexual trauma, from the sins they committed and the sins they were taught. It would create *better men*, both those who had to apologize and others who would learn from seeing it happen.

Not every man could be granted amnesty, of course. Nor would every man be granted forgiveness. There is no path back for the Harvey Weinsteins of the world. There would have been no path back for Jeffrey Epstein. What about Aziz Ansari? The things his accuser says he did on a date with her were wrong. They were damaging. They had hurt someone. They were real, and I am not and will never minimize those things. But were they bad enough to mean he is forever shunned from our society? Is there no path back for him? Could he, with his influence and experience, help in the process of creating better men by becoming a better man, confronting his actions, and asking forgiveness? I don't know, and I won't speak for his victim. But just as there is no path back for the Harvey Weinsteins, there must be a path back for people who are not Harvey Weinstein.

George Floyd was murdered. Breonna Taylor was murdered. Ahmaud Arbery was murdered. Trayvon Martin was murdered. Tamir Rice, Stephon Clark, Rayshard Brooks, Daniel Prude, Atatiana Jefferson, John Crawford, Akai Gurley, Eric Garner. The list goes on and on and on. These are victims of a racist society, perhaps as much as the victims of their killers. Imagine the restorative power of a tribunal where police and others could come forward, to admit what they did, to say it was wrong, to express remorse for that action, and to beg for forgiveness. Imagine what it would mean not only to the families to hear sincere remorse and a prostration before them from the killers of their loved ones, but also to our society, to have a reckoning and a record, a testament of truth, and a place from which we could move forward.

Not every officer will be forgiven. Not every killer will be granted amnesty. Nor should they. But what power the victims would now have thanks to these tribunals. How mighty they would become, armed with the truth and a public record of exactly what happened. How empowering it would be to choose forgiveness—or not—once it was requested. It would restore the people over the politicians, it would take the wind out of the sails of the inherent and structural racism baked all the way into our criminal justice system, and it would open the door for it to be dismantled in the light of truth and honesty and restoration.

Congresswoman Barbara Lee of California has been for years proposing a Truth, Racial Healing, and Transformation Commission. Much like the Truth and Reconciliation Commission in South Africa, this commission would provide the opportunity for a true examination of our racist history and the opportunity to begin to right those wrongs on both systemic and individual levels. Have we ever needed this more in our lifetimes than we need it now? Perhaps those who still remember the evils of legal segregation would have a differing opinion about this, but for most of us, now is the most divided and dangerous time in our memory. Now is when the tectonic plates of our culture are grinding against each other at the epicenter of our societal earth. Now is when we must confront who we are and move toward who we must be. Now is the time to create this commission.

These needs, these desires, these desperate wishes, are not pipe dreams. There are models for them that have already existed, like South Africa's. We have seen them work after unspeakable evils. We have seen the healing they can spur. We can point to the wounds that are not gone but no longer hurt quite so deeply or burn quite as much, and we can attribute that healing to similar commissions. Not just in South Africa: The Nuremberg trials revealed the horrors of the Nazi regime. In Argentina, restorative justice was pursued for those whose loved ones had been "disappeared" by the government. Canada sought to confront its history of the treatment of its First Peoples in its Indian residential schools, and Australia began to confront its treatment of the Aboriginal population there. We can make it work here. We can lift the miasma of guilt and pain and injustice that will linger until we do something.

Some of us can find justice. Others can find forgiveness. All of us can find truth.

When their daughter's killers were granted amnesty for her murder, Linda and Peter Biehl said, "We hope they will receive the support necessary to live productive lives in a non-violent atmosphere. In fact, we hope the spirits of Amy and of those like her will be a force in their new lives."

We have spirits to guide us. We have new lives before us. With reconciliation, we can find a path to the future.

# Divided We Fall

Seventy million people voted for Donald Trump.

After everything he did, after every horrible thing he said, after hundreds of thousands of dead Americans had stacked up at his feet because of his COVID failures, after tens of thousands of proven lies, after the racism and bigotry and flat-out stupidity (yes, I hate that word, but he *wanted to nuke a hurricane,* for fuck's sake) that came from Donald, seventy million American citizens still thought he was the better choice. I can't wrap my brain around it, and that makes it so much harder to figure out how to move forward.

We preach a lot about "hate the ideas, not the person." And I mean it—I really do. But it's hard to forgive when so many people looked at all the evidence and decided that they would try to elect someone who would intentionally endanger and disenfranchise so many people. "I don't like everything he says but he's good for my 401(k)" is the new "I'm not racist, I have Black friends." It's just a ridiculous statement, and it's hard to find a way to see that belief inside a person and not let my fury at those sentiments turn into hate for the individual who carries them.

I'm trying to find a way to let it go. I need to remind myself that many of these people were duped and were victims of the designed division of social media, which profits off of showing us what we want to see, not what actually is true. If people only see statements telling them the sky is orange for years, they will start to believe it. When you show them proof that the sky is blue, the falsehood is so ingrained, so inherent to who they have become, that it is impossible for them to accept reality. Actually, it's worse than that. One side is told by their cult leaders that if the long-accurate, trusted sources of information tell them something, it is certainly false, while only they—their "true" source—provide the truth. So then, when these manipulative media sources say, "Wait, the sky isn't orange, it's green," well, they go right along.

As George Orwell wrote in *Nineteen Eighty-Four,* "The past was alterable. The past never had been altered. Oceania was at war with Eastasia. Oceania had always been at war with Eastasia." We are living in a time of doublethink, and the scariest thing about it is that there is no actual thinking involved. One segment of America has surrendered their thought labor to their idols of misinformation, and I don't know how we get them back.

But if we don't, this is how America falls.

I watched the speech Joe Biden gave when he declared victory, feeling one great weight lift off of me as another settled cold and deep into my chest. There were broad panes of bulletproof glass on either side of the lectern behind which the new president-elect and his family stood as they greeted the crowd. But when he spoke, there was nothing visible in front of him, and I thought of the man who stormed a pizza shop in Washington, DC, with a gun because he had been so deeply programmed by misinformation. I thought of the armed cowards who planned to kidnap Gretchen Whitmer and execute her. I thought of all the sickening work Trump and his regime had done to undermine confidence in American institutions, and the violence that it was inspiring across the country, and I was sick to my stomach. That gap in which the new president-elect was standing looked like an invitation to the vile, anti-American terrorists who stormed the Capitol on January 6 and their hateful ilk.

QAnon and the formerly-fringe-but-now-mainstream right are endangering us all. They reject reality, and outside of our reality, there is no security. The rules of those of us who live in the real world and believe in the Constitution do not matter to these people. They cheered for martial law in order to overturn a free and fair election, and about a third of Congress tried to help them do it when they voted to ignore electoral votes. There is no safety from these people.

Now, I am positive there were other security measures to prevent just the event I worried about from happening, and anyone who saw the new Biden motorcade that night knew that he had the full armor of the presidential protection unit of the Secret Service. He was not in danger. But America definitely is.

There is a group of hundreds of thousands or millions of people here in this nation, entirely detached from reality, being fed lie after lie after lie about the Democrats, and they eat it up as they buy ammo and lovingly polish their M16s. They gather in fields and basements, chat rooms and remote homesteads, and they train. They plot. They seethe. And they hate. They cast themselves as heroes, fan visions of martyrdom, and imagine future history books (in schools where they *pray* before school, goddamn it) proudly listing their names alongside Paul Revere and Sam Adams and George Washington. They believe they are standing up to tyranny when they have more freedom than nearly any person in the world, and someday one of them is going to succeed. Lord knows they have already tried.

We are teeming with Timothy McVeighs, and it will be the end of America if they win.

I believe in America. I believe in the one nation, under God, with liberty and justice for all. But I fear that we are no longer indivisible. No, I fear we are already divided in ways that may be irreparable.

In 2008, a woman approached John McCain at a rally and said that Barack Obama was "an Arab," clearly implying that he was a terrorist. McCain replied, "He's a decent family man and citizen that I just happen to have disagreements with on fundamental issues, and that's what the campaign's all about. He's not." That was it. That was the moment when the American right could have stepped back from the brink and discarded the nonsense and hate, the vitriol and fear. They could have embraced McCain's call for decency and national unity ahead of the opposition of ideas.

They did not. They chose the Tea Party, a roiling mass of anarchy and anger, and espoused a frothy-mouthed rejection of the American identity in favor of power at all costs. It took just eight years (and their hatred of a Black president with an uncommon name) to turn the nation down the path to Gilead. "He's Kenyan," they bleated. "They'll take our guns," they said, quivering, as the NRA crammed that lie down their throats. So they armed up, nearly doubling gun sales in the weeks following Obama's election relative to other presidents. And they kept arming, buying guns at an alarming rate for the entirety of the Obama presidency until there were more guns than people in America, even though those guns are concentrated in only about one-third of American homes. In short, the frightened right stockpiled huge arsenals because a Black man with an African name was elected.

Throughout the Obama presidency, the mechanics of the right wing dug in to allow this divide to fester. Fox News spread the infectious lies, and when they weren't lying *enough*, even farther-right networks sprang up. OANN and Parler corrupted our culture, our truth, our America. People like Marjorie Taylor Greene, who built a profile that got her elected to Congress by spreading these lies, came to the forefront through social media networks that made money on elevating this content. They crammed dirt in the wound, infecting it, poisoning the country. When Ted Kennedy died, the last vestiges of cross-party friendships largely died with him; we lost our last example of being friendly rivals and became bitter enemies. The right found a new buzzword—*socialist*—and burned it into the brains of their followers. They never defined it. In fact, I'd bet if you asked ten thousand people who tweeted the word *socialist* on the right to accurately define socialism and apply it to any Democratic policy, they wouldn't be able to do either. But it didn't matter. Reality was no longer the boundary of discourse. And they had a new shorthand in social media, where quick hits allowed them to get out their message without the need to explain it.

And then, in 2012, Benghazi happened.

Now, it didn't matter that the dozens of investigations continued to find no wrongdoing on the part of anyone in the Obama administration, especially Secretary Clinton. There was no wrongdoing. They knew it. They knew it while they were using it as a bludgeon, and the hate burned through their minions. They were a hornet's nest that had been stirred up by the wind and went looking for someone to sting. America was that someone. Instead of taking a step back when they saw the hatred their rhetoric and lies fomented in the public—and make no mistake, their entire Benghazi hit job was a lie and they knew it—they doubled down over and over and over again, allowing the hatred to wash over them like effluent out of a broken sewer pipe, not caring that they were covered in shit so long as we saw some of it stick to Hillary.

Steve Bannon saw this. And like the opportunistic shit-weasel he is, he went to the person with the least functional moral compass in America: Donald Trump. Trump said to Bannon that he would change his past positions to accommodate a run. But he went so much further than that. He pretended he'd never had them at all. He lied about voting—when and how he voted. As Bob Woodward reported in his first book on the Trump White House, Trump told Steve Bannon he'd hold whatever positions he'd need to hold to win. He was ready to be a completely immaterial reality, a mist of paint blobs ready to blow into whatever picture his base wanted to see. And he did. He bamboozled them completely.

The right elected a man who reflected *who they were* and allowed them to finally show their worst selves to the world with pride. "I'm just like the president," they thought, "so what I think can't be bad." Instead of going to therapy and doing the work, they just put a dark mirror in the White House and strutted in front of it while America withered in the ICU. They cheered as he took everything that was fundamental about being an American and turned it on its head—not refuting the substance of arguments but refuting that the arguments even existed. We'd show them video evidence of Trump doing and saying things and they'd yell, "Fake news." Even when it came from the lips of their cult leader himself, they refused to believe it unless he said it was the gospel truth.

It's hard not to hate them.

It's hard to remember to hate the idea and not the person.

See, I *am* a patriot. I love everything about the American idea. And I've watched these people just giddily throw gasoline onto the burning house of our nation and then look me in the eye and say *I* did it, while the dripping gas can was still in their hand.

So I breathe. It's hard not to hate them, but I don't. I understand they have been manipulated. I understand that they have done damage that we might not be able to fix, but I also understand they were duped into believing they were helping the nation. I know they, right now, are not capable of seeing their own doublethink. I know they believe we have always been at war with Eastasia. I know they believe war is peace, freedom is slavery, ignorance is strength, because that is all they see in their social media feed. I remember Jesus on the cross. "Father, forgive them, for they know not what they do."

But it's hard.

And now we have a moment. We have another opportunity here to step back from the brink. Will there be anyone on the right, any single leader of strength and integrity, who can reestablish reality in the minds of their followers? Will someone arise for the Republicans like JFK and LBJ rose and forced the Democrats to try to right our horrible wrongs on civil rights and racial justice? Is there anyone waiting in the wings to push back on the bigotry and fear and disinformation of the right and the fringe right? Will nobody disavow OANN and Breitbart? Will nobody spank Ben Shapiro, the weaselly little mouthpiece of alt-right outlets like Breitbart and *The Daily Wire*, and put him to bed without supper? Isn't there anyone besides Mitt Romney and a smattering of House members on that side of the aisle who will stand up

and loudly say Donald Trump is bad for America and we
need to pump the brakes fast?

Time will tell.

In the meantime, I worry we're all me, watching Biden's
speech and seeing so much potential and so much danger. I
hope things go the right way.

# United We Stand

Seventy million people voted for Donald Trump.

After everything he did, after every horrible thing he said, after hundreds of thousands of dead Americans had stacked up at his feet because of his COVID failures, after tens of thousands of proven lies, after the racism and bigotry and flat-out stupidity (yes, I hate that word, but he *wanted to nuke a hurricane,* for fuck's sake) that came from Donald, seventy million American citizens still thought he was the better choice. I can't wrap my brain around it, and that makes it so much harder to figure out how to move forward.

I watched the speech Joe Biden gave when he declared victory, feeling one great weight lift off of me as another settled cold and deep into my chest. There were broad panes of bulletproof glass on either side of the lectern behind which the new president-elect and his family stood as they greeted the crowd. But when he spoke, there was nothing visible in front of him, and I thought of the man who stormed a pizza shop in Washington, DC, with a gun because he had been so deeply programmed by misinformation. I thought of the armed cowards who planned to kidnap Gretchen Whitmer and execute her. I thought of all the sickening work Trump and his regime had done to undermine confidence in American institutions, and the violence that it was inspiring across the country, and I was sick to my stomach. That gap in which the new president-elect was standing looked like an invitation.

Joe Biden celebrated onstage with his family, with Vice President–Elect Harris and her family, and watched an amazing fireworks and light show. People gathered at a drive-in rally, socially distanced and safe from the virus, honking their horns and dancing in their seats and on the roofs of their cars, as people in cities across America took to the streets in peaceful celebration. And that's what it was—a celebration. Of course, I was writing this the day after the race was called, after which Trump's "army" materialized. There have been violent clashes with the police, there have been violent clashes with conspiracy theorists, and there has been no serious indication that violence is going away. But I can't live without allowing myself to hope that there is a path forward where people heal.

President-Elect Biden is a healer. That was the theme that ran through the event on the night the election was called and he emerged victorious. There was no gloating. No victory lap. He spoke of his faith, paraphrasing the Bible: "The Bible tells us that to everything there is a season," he said, "a time to build, a time to reap, a time to sow. And a time to heal. This is the time to heal in America."

I cried hot, fat tears when he said that, as knots I'd been holding in for four years loosened and blood began to flow to places in my body that had been blocked off since that horrible night Trump was elected. It was a catharsis—for me, for our nation, and for the world. And the world responded, with people in cities across the globe reveling with us in our return to something normal and humane. Church bells rang across Paris; there were fireworks in London. Our allies rejoiced as stable, competent governance made its way back into the world's most powerful nation. Our allies remembered our friendship even though we had treated them so poorly those past few years.

The world began to heal, and perhaps the nation as well.

While the Republicans currently in office have largely been silent or complicit in perpetuating the dangerous farce of election fraud, those who came before have been speaking out loudly and clearly in support of a transition of power. President George W. Bush, with whom I agree on almost nothing, released a powerful and moving statement congratulating President-Elect Biden, acknowledging the history made by Vice President–Elect Harris, focusing on the American ideals of democracy and unity. Michael Steele, former RNC chair, celebrated, as did Joe Walsh, a former GOP congressman. David Frum, the former Bush speechwriter who coined the phrase "Axis of Evil," marveled at the joy and kindness in Washington, tweeting, "I have never seen DC drivers so politely let cars into the flow of traffic ahead of them." And former Republican presidential nominee Mitt Romney—the only current high office–holder of the bunch—wished our nation's new leaders well and offered his prayers and support.

Granted, each of these prominent Republicans has a history with Trump. But each of them represents something to which we can return. Each of them is a person I would fight (and have fought) with on so many policy issues, but I've also had conversations with several of them that let me know I could also sit across the table from them and enjoy their company. They were not my enemies; they were my philosophical rivals. Their leadership now, I hope, will be the spark that allows others to follow them out of the dark night our nation has found herself in.

And here's what our side has to be ready to do: We need to meet in the middle. Unity cannot only happen if people can pass an ideological purity test identifying who is a good human and who is a bad human. Of course there are lines, but our line shouldn't be "That person supports eliminating the estate tax, they're on the bad list forever." We need to convince our opponents that they are wrong, not demonize them for disagreeing. We can win on our ideas, but nobody will listen if we call the person who wants to eliminate an inheritance tax a fascist. We need to rein in and redirect the fringe of our party that goes to protests for the purpose of engaging in conflict with police. (I want to be clear here that I am *not* speaking about protesters who erupted in rage at the killings of George Floyd, Trayvon Martin, Breonna Taylor, Michael Brown, and so many more. I *am* talking about the handful of people on our side who showed up at election celebrations with gas masks and shields.) We need to find a way to discuss and disagree rather than demonize and hate. We need to be who we wish *they* would be.

It won't be easy. It feels like anger is burned into our national soul. It feels like our opponents are our enemies. It feels like they hate us, so we should hate them. But I'm trying to take my cues from Joe Biden here. We choose not to cooperate. We choose to hate. We can choose the other path, the harder but more rewarding path. We can pull back from insults and offer invitations. We can be Americans before Democrats. Patriots before Republicans. We can *choose* to be better than we have been.

This does not mean we overlook the past. This does not mean we extend the hand of friendship to the people who put hate into policy. We're not going to be nice to Trump or Mitch McConnell, and I want every person who broke the law in Trump's administration tried. There are legitimately bad people who have done legitimately bad things, and the only place they have in our history is *in our history*. They have forfeited their place in our present, and the last chance they have at a "patriot act" is to amble quietly away into obscurity. But we have to separate those people—the Stephen Millers who wrote hateful and racist immigration policies, and the Ken Cuccinellis who gleefully enforced them from positions of power in the Trump regime—from Bob down the street with a Trump flag and a different viewpoint. We have to open our hearts to conversation and to really, really hearing *why* they believe the things they do. That's how we move that needle. We have to have uncomfortable conversations and find revolutionary solutions.

I've tried to get there before. I sat in Ted Cruz's office and pleaded with him to do *something* about gun violence in America. I brought my friend Fred Guttenberg with me to share his pain, and he did. Fred showed Senator Cruz photos of his daughter's body in the hallways of Marjory Stoneman Douglas High School and tried to dispel the misinformation the right spreads about gun violence prevention measures. We took a lot of heat from our side for that meeting and did not change Cruz's mind. But we had a cordial discussion, and one thing you might never know unless you've been to his office is that his staff is full of the sweetest people you'll ever meet. I guarantee you that before I walked into that office, they saw me as evil. I know in my heart I was ready for them to be. But we came away with a different impression of one another, I hope. I know I did. Of course, over the year that followed, Ted Cruz decided to turn even harder to the right and has since shown his true anti-American colors. But in that moment, there was just the faintest glimmer of a humanity I had not previously sensed.

I'm still pretty pissed at Ted Cruz for how he continued to support Trump through his war on our republic. Ted's not a stupid man; he knew exactly what he was doing and he did it anyway. I don't know if it's for power or leverage or what, but he hung in with this abuser, the man who mocked his family while campaigning and cracked the pillars of American democracy. It makes me sad, mostly. But I do know this—I'd go back and have that conversation every single time. If we only talk to people who agree with us, we will never make any progress. If we only shout at people who disagree with us, we will never make any progress.

I sat with staff in Lisa Murkowski's office and found a whole lot of common ground. And I've had conversations with some of the prominent Republicans I previously mentioned on my podcast or other programs. I thought I would find that we could only discover common ground on Trump—none of them are fans, and I knew that going into the discussions. But we opened a lot of ground on a number of issues. Gun violence prevention, violence against women, COVID, international relations. We might not have agreed down to the letter, but we certainly were on the same playing field instead of opposite trenches in a battle. Senator Murkowski and her staff were willing to engage on gun violence prevention, the Equal Rights Amendment, and other issues I hold dear. I would never have thought I would have said this before talking with them, but those conversations were inspiring. They were uplifting. They reminded me that the things that bring us together are often greater than those that divide us. It's a cliché, often used to try to shut down important disagreements, but it's also true, and I am grateful for that truth.

Each side will say they are Abel, but we each have a little bit of Cain in us. We are our brothers' keepers. We are bound together even in the most difficult times. We share a land and the common bond of a nation. We are responsible for our shared well-being, and usually what is good for them is good for me. I want your kids to have good, safe schools. You want my kids to have clean air and water. I want our police to be safe on the job. You want children of all colors to be safe in their communities. I want everyone to have an equal playing field in America and equal access to opportunity. So do you. And so do they. I believe this to be true. It *has* to be true, or we're doomed.

Unity does not mean homogeneity. It does not mean we all think alike or act alike. Abraham Lincoln, one of the greatest political writers in history, wrote the following in his second annual address to Congress:

> *Will not the good people respond to a united, and earnest appeal from us? Can we, can they, by any other means, so certainly, or so speedily, assure these vital objects? We can succeed only by concert. It is not "can any of us imagine better?" but, "can we all do better?" The dogmas of the quiet past, are inadequate to the stormy present. The occasion is piled high with difficulty, and we must rise—with the occasion. As our case is new, so we must think anew, and act anew. We must disenthrall ourselves, and then we shall save our country.*
>
> *Fellow-citizens, we cannot escape history. We of this Congress and this administration, will be remembered in spite of ourselves. No personal significance, or insignificance, can spare one or another of us. The fiery trial through which we pass, will light us down, in honor or dishonor, to the latest generation. We say we are for the Union. The world will not*

*forget that we say this. We know how to save the Union. The*
*world knows we do know how to save it. We—even we here—*
*hold the power, and bear the responsibility.*

The dogmas of our generation's quiet past are inadequate to the stormy present. Has there ever been a more prescient line written for our times? Has there ever been a stronger call to reject that which divides us? Republicans revere Lincoln. Democrats revere Lincoln. For all of his plodding slowness, for all his equivocations on the issue of slavery, he fought to preserve a union and advance the ideas of freedom in a time when freedom had a much, much deeper meaning to far too many in our nation. It took a war, but they found their way back to unity.

I pray we can do the same with just an election.

# The Future

My granddaughter sits on my lap, smoothing the wrinkles that now carve their way from my eyes, tracing them as though they were a map of the struggles that came before her. She finds her way down my cheeks, Bella watching from across the room with the mischief that always glowed behind her eyes still there, remembering how she used to do this with me. Birds sing in the backyard, where Milo and my nephew Luke are sharing a beer and tending to the horses while David sets up Saturday sandwiches.

It's a tradition we kept, and it's perfect.

I am happy.

But the world is ... mixed.

We had to move from California when the fires refused to give up. My canyon, once full of bright greens and woodland smells, turned into a tinderbox around 2030. Too little water.

Too much heat. Not enough action. It was the dust bowl in reverse, and we joined the masses moving from the coast to the interior of the country, where the rain still fell and the sky never glowed orange save for a spectacular sunset. Not now, not yet, anyway. We could hear the creek running still, even during dry months. There were a lot of dry months, too many, but water enough to fend them off still. I didn't know how long it would last. Certainty was a thing of the past, before the fires. People used to joke that California was going to fall into the ocean because of the earthquakes. Now we joked that we wished it would, just to put out the constant inferno. But nobody laughed.

I know how lucky we were to be able to get out, to be able to buy a new home, to be able to start anew. It's not what we once had, but as I look around at my family, here, together, it is enough. It has to be.

All around us the land is flat. Tall cornfields stretch as far as we can see, surrounded by sharp barbed wire and useless scarecrows. I'm not sure why they use scarecrows anymore, since the crows migrated north. The good corn is in Canada now, and so are they. Our corn is still edible, but the anti-crow modifications to its genetic code made it taste less sweet, and the dry weather made it less juicy. We still slather it with butter and sprinkle it with salt, but it's an echo of a past that is gone forever. It is a reminder of our failures. It is America.

The warm, dry breeze causes a susurrus to rise from the field, green leaves whispering to each other the words of the wind. I think it tells us of hope. The greatest and most terrible word in English, that. It allows us to move forward. It gives us the courage to fight. It tempts us and crushes us. It is an elevator missing a cable, missing stops and swaying dangerously as it carries us upward tenuously, slowly, dizzyingly. It could plummet at any minute, and we would be destroyed, but it is the only elevator we have. The only path to the top. The only way out. Hope.

Dare I listen?

I used to hear crickets when I listened. They're gone now with the crows.

But the warmth of my granddaughter, her soft and playful hands exploring my face, reminds me that all is not lost. She wasn't supposed to be. She wouldn't have been, if not for the universal medical care we enacted. My family has always had the resources to provide for ourselves, including medically. But the investment America made in medicine, in providing free and excellent care to everyone, spurred a renaissance in the field. Massive cash infusions from the government and from the private sector led to incredible breakthroughs that made formerly impossible illnesses now easy to cure. The hands on my face were proof.

When we found out that Bella's college roommate was

pregnant, David and I rejoiced. Sophie was like a daughter to us, and when she lost her parents in the unrest, we took her in as our own. We had lost so much personally and collectively when we lost California. We were mired in that loss, trying desperately to keep our chins up and go on, but it was *hard*. Every day we remembered what we no longer had, wishing for the view across the canyon and the easy trip to the ocean. At night, I had to stop using an ocean soundtrack to lull me to sleep because the ocean was more than a thousand miles away now, and I didn't know if I would ever put my feet in the Pacific again. The thought made me too sad to even listen to a recording.

But when that call came, the rickety hope elevator that had been stuck for so long shot up, straight, smooth, and true. We recommitted to each other, to the world. We wanted to find ways to undo the things that had gone wrong and build a world our grandchild—blood or not—would be safe in and proud of. We wished hard, we laughed harder, and we loved the hardest.

When Sophie called months later to tell us that the tests had come back with abnormalities, the cable snapped and we plummeted. David despaired. I raged. I was so pissed. At God, at the nature of things, at every loss. But new breakthroughs, miracles of tiny technology I never could have dreamed of when I was Sophie's age, took hold, and the pudgy result is on my lap getting ready for nap time. Miracles are real. Anything is possible. Hope springs eternal.

Drums start crashing from the basement, and I know Milo is teaching Luke a new drum riff. They've kept that up together since Milo stopped touring. Concert tours aren't all that common anymore. Virtual is cheaper. Virtual is safer. We learned our lessons, finally, and big crowds are exceedingly rare anymore. It gives me so much happiness to hear them together, carrying on the tradition of music and love for drumming that has been so important to my family. We carry songs with us from the past and use them to tell stories to the future. It's been that way since we evolved into humans. If it ever stops being that way, we will no longer be humans. It's part of who we are, and the cacophony of weaving that tapestry fills my house with rhythmic bangs and crashes, and I love it.

I don't know what's left. I know we didn't get enough right, and I can't say what twenty years from now will look like, or if I will even be here to see it. But what I do know is there is hope in this house and all that comes with our family. There is a future before us, and a future beyond that. The choices we make, the wrinkles we earn, each twists that future a little. Everything we do, every choice we make, turns things to the better or to the worse. As I feel my granddaughter nestling into my shoulder, sleep heavy in her slowing hands, I hope I've made the right choices. And I hope she will make even better choices than I did.

Hope.

=

# A Survivor's Prayer

If only
If only I could:
Save you
Help you
Remove that weight from your tired shoulders,
and become the joy of an unburdened you
I would.
From Her Too and Him Too,
I would remove you from that particular we,
and lift that heavy hashtag from in front of you.
Four perpendicular slashes
of one size fits all
should not fit you.
Me too.
I am you.

I said, "I am you."

And I will carry your weight, I carry it already.

Together up the mountain every day until together we
      find ourselves

together at the bottom each morning.

Sisyphus sisters.

We are the ephemeral queens of Ephyra:

more than you insinuate:

we cheat you by surviving.

We are here.

Arm in arm.

Whisper your stories on the mountain,

Their sound shields us all.

If only I could save you.

If only I could take it away.

If only I could help you.

If only I could I could cure yesterday.

It starts with "we" before all "too"s.

We weep, we shake, in the same worn shoes.

One size fits all of awe and pain

One decibel of thunder, a lifetime of rain.

I am you.

I said, "I am you."

I carry your weight.

We are more than committees, those committers of hate.

I am bonded to you, arm in arm

Until we live in a world with no sexual harm.

Protect us by listening. Protect us forever.

Because we are here. Uprising together.

# Acknowledgments

A book like this does not come to be on its own, and I would be remiss to miss thanking some of the many people who helped make it possible.

My literary agent, Molly Glick, and her team worked so hard to help me find a home for this book, and I am very grateful. John Parsley, Jill Schwartzman, and the entire team at Dutton made it much better than it otherwise would have been, and any oversights in the editorial work belong to me and not them.

My entire family carried me as I worked on this, as they do in all my other work. Without you, I don't know who I am. Thank you.

I've spent years—and especially the last half decade or so—deep in the trenches with amazing activists committed to changing the world. Every day you inspire me and challenge me to do better. Never stop.

And, finally, to the 81,232,916 of you who voted to kick Donald Trump out on his ass, the whole world owes you a debt of gratitude.

# About the Author

**Alyssa Milano** is an actor, producer, host, activist, entrepreneur, humanitarian, and *New York Times* bestselling author. She also hosts and produces the successful podcast *Sorry Not Sorry*. Her four-book middle-grade series with Scholastic began with the bestselling *Hope: Project Middle School*, with the fourth book, *Hope: Project Go Green*, published in April 2021. Milano starred on the long-running series *Charmed* and *Who's the Boss?* and has appeared in more than twenty films over the course of her career. As an activist, Milano chooses to shine a spotlight on causes that matter deeply to her. Her advancement of #MeToo sparked a viral movement of women fighting against sexual harassment and assault. She is active on the ERA Coalition's Advisory Council. She is also the ACLU's Ambassador for Reproductive Rights. In the wake of the mass shooting at Marjory Stoneman Douglas High School, Milano became one of the founders of #NoRA, a coalition dedicated to combating the NRA money in political campaigns. For fifteen years, she has been a UNICEF National Ambassador. She has lobbied members of Congress for greater rights for immigrants as well as education reform and has been on the forefront of efforts to protect health coverage for all Americans.